After the Murder of My Son

AFTER THE MURDER OF MY SON

MARY RONDEAU WESTRA

Denny —

After all these years, what a joy to meet again —

Mary

9-8-10

NORTH STAR PRESS OF ST. CLOUD, INC.
St. Cloud, Minnesota

ISBN: 0-87839-398-6

ISBN-13: 978-0-87839-398-5

First Edition, September 1, 2010

Printed in the United States of America

Published by

North Star Press of St. Cloud, Inc.

P.O. Box 451

St. Cloud, Minnesota 56302

www.northstarpress.com

For Mark, Carolyn, and Ann, with all my love

Table of Contents

Someone I loved once gave me
A box full of darkness.
It took me years to understand
That this, too, was a gift.
—Mary Oliver, *Thirst*

Life is a sorrowful joy, and a joyful sorrow.
—Joseph Campbell

Ann, Peter, and Carolyn on a surfboard on White Bear Lake.

On the Dock

I come to this dock to try to breathe. I step off the narrow patch of rocky shoreline, tread the dock's narrow planks, and plop my tired body onto the humble bench at the end. My breath slows as my eyes track the aqua ripples stippled with white across the water's surface and gaze miles beyond to the tree-lined shore, the horizon, and the cloud-streaked sky. Searching the expanse, I think about how this old wood dock has seen a family grow and die, regroup, and come to life again.

Carolyn was four, Peter, eight, and Ann nearly ten, when we moved to the sturdy house at the top of the hill. We've had such fun here . . . my family . . . I and Mark, to whom I've been married now for more than forty years, and our three kids. I used to haul air-pots of lemonade and colanders of fresh grapes down to the dock to watch my children play in the lake while I sat on the dock. I remember Carolyn and a friend propping the board of an old windsurfer against the dock's bench and shushing into six-foot deep water as though they were at a water park, splashing water on the board to keep it slick and fast. When Peter came down, they tossed the surfboard into the water and played king of the mountain, elbowing and pushing each other in order to be the last one standing on the bobbing board.

Once during that first summer I panicked when Ann and her friend disappeared from the dock, leaving behind their towels and inner tubes. I called the fire department, only to find the girls a quarter mile down the shore in her friend's pool. They'd floated there on air mattresses.

Boats were part of every balmy weekend. Ann and Peter learned to sail in a little two-sailed scow leased from the nearby yacht club. They raced in regattas, Peter as the captain while his older sister, Ann, was crew. On Sundays we'd pack our breakfast in a basket and go out on our speedboat, find a quiet bay, and jump into the water when we got hot.

By the age of twelve Peter was a graceful and avid water-skier. He'd sit on the edge of the dock, slip his foot into his own slalom ski, leap into the water, and return to the dock without even getting wet. In high school, he'd often come home late in the evening to take his friends on the boat for a moonlight cruise.

Now I'm warm with sun and memories that both sear and calm. I move from the dock's bench to the stubby-legged beach chair, straighten my legs, and close my eyes. I can see those little kids playing in the water, splashing and kicking with friends. I can see us in the boat, hauling kids around the lake on tubes, carving circle after circle as they squeal for sharper turns. And looking back over my shoulder to the grassy yard, I can see the big kids kneeling in pyramids on the trampoline under the shade of huge century-old cottonwood trees.

I can also see a pack of twenty-somethings hovering around a bonfire to mark the death of my son.

Part One
Murder

One

July 8, 2001

I t was a hot and humid morning when the phone rang at seven. Mark and I were asleep near the open front door, our bed moved to the front foyer because we were remodeling upstairs. I got out of bed and went into the kitchen to answer.

"Is this the Washington County sheriff's office?" asked the man on the other end.

"No," I said.

"Is this 651-426-...?" sounding as if he were reading from a slip of paper.

"Yes."

Then he hung up.

My breathing stopped. My body went rigid and cold. I stared at the phone. Something told me this hadn't been just a wrong number. I remembered hearing that when something really awful happens, the sheriff doesn't tell you over the phone. He comes to your house.

I climbed back into bed, jostled Mark, but he brushed me off, told me to go back to sleep. I lay awake and waited. I listened to the cars on the road outside. I waited for one to come up our driveway. I watched the clock ... ten minutes ... twenty minutes.

Seven-thirty ... still no sheriff's car. Maybe I was wrong. Or maybe the work shift changed at eight and someone would come then. So I waited, unable to leave the bed. Mark got up, put on his bike clothes, and started to read the paper at the kitchen table. He called out, "Are you coming, Mary? It'll get too hot, you know, if we wait too long."

I dragged myself out of bed, put on my bike clothes, and told myself not to worry. I was sitting at the bottom of the kitchen steps, bending over to buckle my bike shoe . . . another minute and we'd be gone . . . when the door bell rang. The sound of it was a kick in the gut.

Shivering and shaking, whimpering, I headed through the kitchen toward the front door. As soon as I caught the glimpse of blue on the other side of the screen door, I stopped . . . and I screamed for Mark.

He was right behind me, pushing past me, angry already. "What do you want?" he yelled at the two men at the door. In a flash, I knew that something awful, really awful, had happened to one of my children. My mind raced through their whereabouts. Twenty-year-old Carolyn, on summer break from college in Maine, was in the Boundary Waters Canoe Area, leading a group of teenaged girls from a YMCA camp. Ann, twenty-six, had left Long Island to drive home to Baltimore where she was attending medical school. Maybe she was still on the road, I worried. Twenty-four-year-old Peter was at a bachelor party with his buddies in Atlantic City, New Jersey. We never worried about him.

"Can we come in?" asked the man in a clerical collar with a white beard.

"No, you can't!" bellowed Mark. "Tell me what you have to say right now!"

In the gentlest of voices, through the screen door, the clerical collar said, "Your son's been killed. He was kicked by bouncers outside a bar in Atlantic City."

We collapsed onto the bed next to the front door.

The two men let themselves into the house. On the bed by the door, Mark tucked into a fetal position, howled. I encircled his body, laid my head on his back, began to sob. One of the men asked whom they should call. I stammered, trying to recall a couple names, blanked, but somehow directed them to our address book. "Second drawer on the left, by the door to the family room."

Within minutes, Steve and Shelley, friends with five grown children and grandchildren nearly as old as our own kids, crouched by the side of the bed. Pat came from down the street. When the sheriff asked me about a relative, I told him to call Mark's sister Ruth.

Then the men in blue suits went away, leaving a card on the kitchen counter.

My mind was blank. I couldn't move. I couldn't think. Pat asked if she should call our pastors, call our friends. I didn't know what to say. Somehow I sensed this moment of quiet would soon cease, our house would overflow, and I wasn't ready. Leave me alone, world. Stay away. I need to think. I don't want a bunch of women keening over me . . . not yet.

I called Charlie, my bosom buddy, who used to live with her husband, Bob, down the street from our last home, whose son had played with Peter in grade school.

"I'm coming, Mary, I'm coming," she said as soon as she heard my voice, already having been called by Shelley.

Yankton, where Charlie and Bob lived, was five hours from the Twin Cities. "Hurry, Charlie. Please hurry. And bring Bob. Mark needs him."

I called Mark's sister Ruth again. "Come right away." Duluth, where Ruth lived, was two hours away.

"Yes, call our pastors," I told Pat. "But don't let them make an announcement in church. Not yet. The girls . . . I've got to get the girls."

Ann didn't answer her cell phone. It felt like hours before she groggily did answer. I blurted out, "Peter's been killed. He's been kicked to death by bouncers. Come home!" Just like that . . . so blunt. I wonder now how else I could have said it. I remember her exact response: "Oh my God, how awful." I hung up and left her on her own to figure out how to get home. Luckily Steve stepped in and booked her flight, thinking for me and taking care of my daughter when I couldn't.

The camp staff couldn't find Lyn. She had departed a couple days before on a trip with beginning paddlers, but the group hadn't followed the scheduled route. Fellow leaders, Lyn's friends, set out in canoes to find her.

I was still in my bike clothes, still in stocking feet. The house was filling with people, everyone hugging me, women keening over me. A few were in golf clothes, golf shoes, coming from the course as soon as they heard. I looked at my watch . . . only ten-thirty in the morning. Already it was the longest day of my life.

Mark called Peter's cell phone. Peter's friend Pete Steinberg answered immediately, as though he were waiting for the call. "What happened, Pete?"

Mark listened for a long time. I heard him ask about the party, about the bar, about the drinking. I heard him ask if there were any drugs, not that there's been the slightest hint of drugs, ever, with Peter. No, Steinberg answered, there were no drugs. They were partying late. Peter was drunk. Without provocation, for no reason he could tell, Steinberg said, a bouncer took Peter out of the bar at about four in the morning, roughed him up, left him, and went back into the bar. Steinberg had followed the bouncer and Peter out of the club and witnessed the attack, but he was not able to prevent it. Steinberg said Peter was mad and had tried to go back in, but when he opened the door, he was met by several men streaming out the door.

Peter and Steinberg were both knocked to the pavement, but it was Peter who the five men proceeded to kick in the head and torso. Steinberg said he crawled and threw his body onto Peter's, covering his head. Eventually the men went back into the bar, leaving my son unresponsive on the pavement. Steinberg began CPR, knowing how to not cause greater injury because he was in med school, and then hailed down a passing patrol car. When the paramedics arrived to take Peter to the hospital, Steinberg was not allowed to go along. Our son was declared dead within the hour.

That was the extent of the information we had. Our son was dead. The life-changing information had to sink in before we could frame any questions. Questions were not yet important.

My sister called. Sixteen months younger than I, Nancy and I had never been close. She called from her home on the other side of the city after hearing from my mother that Peter had been in an auto accident. "No, it wasn't an auto accident." Then Nancy peppered me with questions: "What happened? Aren't you angry? What are you going to do? Are you calling an attorney? What do you need?" I felt pushed. I didn't have a clue what I needed or what I was going to do. I was short with her. She got shards of anger, already lurking, ready to spike through the shock of the morning. Nancy didn't come to the house that day. Instead she left on her scheduled vacation up north, and I didn't see her until the day of the visitation.

Mark was on and off the phone all day. He sat at the round table in our family room, pads of post-its piling up, phone cord stretched through glass doors from the kitchen to his command post. From camp, he heard they'd sent out a float plane to look for Lyn's group. From the Atlantic County District Attorney, he learned a criminal investigation was underway. Then he called the mortician who used to live next door.

Mark stood up and said to me, "Mary, this is going to get really ugly. They were at a strip club, you know."

I was stunned, horrified. I squeezed my eyes shut, shook my head slowly from side to side. My son at a strip club? Why? What sort of entertainment . . . ? Even in those earliest moments, though I wasn't really aware of it then, I felt a glimmer of embarrassment and a shred of concern for what people were going to think of my son. But I caught myself, hoisted up my shoulders, and vowed to immediately steel my heart.

Oh God, whatever! What difference does Peter being at a strip club make now? He's dead! His being in a sordid place didn't mean he was doing anything wrong.

In a flash, I vowed to be proud of Peter, no matter what. I would back him up, defend him. I would honor him. I would guard his reputation, no matter what we learned, no matter what had happened.

Please, dear God, help me.

Our pastors, Darlene and Linda, came when church concluded. The kitchen was crowded with knots of people, Mark standing in one corner, encircled by friends, me huddled in another. I felt far away from my partner, helpless to get to his side. At first it was mostly women, but then men started to come. Conversation was muted. No one asked questions, at least not of us. Rather, everyone talked about the last time they had seen Peter, how great he had looked, how friendly, how happy, how much he seemed to like his job. I felt embraced by a thousand arms, sustained . . . but still close to collapse. Just when I felt I might fall, I noticed warm banana bread and soft butter on the corner of the kitchen counter. Manna from heaven, the first food I'd had all day. It was nearly six o'-clock.

The float plane had located Lyn's group in late afternoon. She was packing up her stuff and would be home in a few hours. We learned later that her group of beginning paddlers had shortened their route. The campers were setting up the tents, and Lyn and her co-leader were taking turns swimming and cooking when they noticed the float plane circling above. Through a megaphone the pilot asked their names and then told Lyn to call camp. Cell phone reception was weak. She heard only that her brother was dead, but she had no idea why.

As Ruth was leaving for the airport to pick up Ann, I ran out after her and hopped into her car. On instinct I knew I had to be the first to embrace my firstborn child. I remembered how scared and lonely I felt flying home, years earlier, when my eldest sister, Betty, had died of an overdose of pills. Newly married but alone because Mark was in the Navy, I was terrified then of what I'd find in the childhood home I had always taken for granted, with parents I'd always considered unflappable. But my mother was too preoccupied to make a fuss over me, so I made a bed for myself on the floor of my father's den. I didn't feel ignored, I felt self-reliant. My sister Nancy, however, told me later she had felt abandoned by her parents at a time when she sorely needed them.

Ann looked forlorn and scared coming off the plane. She fell into my arms. I immediately felt thirty years younger, wishing I hadn't been alone on that plane coming back to Minnesota when my sister had died. I resolved then to take care of my daughters.

Back home, Bob and Charlie arrived from Yankton. With dusk the house got quiet. An eery, unsettled stillness ended our day of hell. We waited for Lyn in the dark, Mark and I and Ann lying on the bed by the front door, Charlie and Bob resting in the family room.

About two o'clock in the morning, we heard the chug of the camp van coming up our driveway. We raced outside as Lyn tumbled out the door. We scooped her into our arms. We were one huge sobbing circle, Mark, me, and Ann, Charlie and Bob, and Lyn and her friends—including Kris, Peter's best high school buddy, who was on the camp's staff. He was the one who had met Lyn when she returned to camp, gave her some details, and helped her pack up. When the van left, we went back inside, and I asked Bob to say a prayer. Then he and Charlie departed to spend the night with Shelley and Steve. Just four of us remained—for the first time—our new family. Smaller, stranger, but so permanent. We lay together for several hours on the bed next to the open front door, then moved from bed to bed for the remainder of the night, determined to stay tight and close to each other.

Two

Week Before

P eter had just been home, looking so good, so grown up, so ready
to take on life, so eager to see his family and friends. I had picked
him up at the airport only eight days earlier.

"Hi Mom!" he called as he burst through the open glass doors of
the international terminal at the Minneapolis-St. Paul airport. All six feet,
three inches of his broad-shouldered, trim body in sneakers, rumpled
khakis, and navy T-shirt bounded out, suit bag on one shoulder, laptop
hanging from the other, golf bag pushed out in front of his body. I had to
stretch to hug him even though I'm tall too. He felt strong, warm. He
yawned a couple times as we headed to the car, telling me he slept through
most of the flight since he hadn't gone to bed the night before. He and
Mac had hosted a party in their flat, so he had stayed awake to clean up
before his early morning departure.

Two years out of college, Peter had been working as an investment banker in London for the past six months. He returned home for his
grandmother's—my mother's—ninetieth birthday celebration. He would
spend a week at our home in Dellwood, on the eastern shore of White
Bear Lake, and then leave for Atlantic City to meet college friends for a
bachelor party. Brad, his roommate during his sophomore year at Middlebury College in Vermont, would be the first of the gang to get married,
and Peter was going to be a groomsman.

We hopped into Mark's '92 green Saab convertible, lowered the top,
and headed home. Mark was in Montana with real-estate clients for some

Our family on July 1, 2001, my mother's ninetieth birthday.

fly-fishing, a first effort at what would become his saving passion. He would join us the next day for my mother's party. I drove us home so Peter could call his friend Todd to make plans for later in the evening. Peter and I would play some golf in the late afternoon.

As soon as he changed into shorts and put in his contacts, we headed to the nearby yacht club. We'd been members there since Ann and Peter, while in college, had taken up golf more seriously and urged us to make it a family activity. When he was the new kid in the neighborhood, Peter had caddied at the club. He started to play there and got his first set of clubs from one of the men for whom he caddied. A natural athlete, Peter was good at golf. He played a lot at Middlebury's course, we'd hear later.

Neither Peter nor I played well that afternoon, but we laughed. He high-fived my good shots, took his own shots in stride, and didn't seem to get riled by his drives like he used to. He's grown-up, I thought. We quit after six holes, called it practice, and promised to play more rounds during the week. Then we met for a casual supper on the clubhouse porch with Carolyn, a nongolfer, who'd driven from camp that morning for her grandmother's birthday, and Bente, Steve and Shelley's daughter, home from Washington DC, who had always been a friend to all three of my kids.

Sitting around with these young people on the clubhouse porch, I felt relaxed, content. No one seemed to be in any hurry. Peter's friend Todd showed up just in time for dessert. I felt included, like one of them, or more like the queen bee, listening to the four fresh-faced kids in their early twenties bantering away about their jobs and their classes, sharing and connecting with each other over brownie sundaes.

The next day, Sunday, July 1, we prepared for my mother's birth-day party. Ann hadn't intended to be there. Despite my exhortations— "You've got to be here! All the cousins are coming! Grandma's turning ninety, after all!"—she had decided a three-week-long backpacking trip out west was more important because she might not have time again dur-ing med school and residency for such a long vacation. But then she called to say they had come off the trail because her back hurt and her friend Stephanie couldn't carry more stuff. The two girls drove all night and crashed on mattresses I had laid on the living room floor, Ann's bedroom too disheveled by the remodeling for them to sleep in it. They got up just in time to shower and dress for the party.

Striding into the ground-floor entertainment center of my mom's building, flanked by my three handsome kids, I felt like a peacock. I wore a flouncy, flowered gauze skirt and a fuchsia-colored silk sweater, topped off with a broad-brimmed beflowered hat I'd worn for a recent donor event at the museum where I worked in fundraising. Ann, who resembles me and is nearly as tall, wore a simple short khaki skirt and black knit top, her shoulder-length brown hair tucked behind her ears, her face plain but for a touch of lipstick. Lyn, shorter and more muscled, looked a bit uncomfortable in her sister's borrowed calf-length black knit dress. Her short curly hair was barretted down, her legs shaved for the first time in months. Peter wore a light-blue buttoned-down oxford-cloth shirt and khaki pants. His hands were tucked in his pockets.

Family gatherings were often awkward for me. I felt estranged from my sisters; sometimes we didn't talk for months. We had come together— all of us, including my deceased sister's kids from Canada—only twice in twenty years: once when my father died of cancer in 1981, and again when my mom turned eighty. Lyn was the youngest of the cousins then. Pictures show her ten-year-old's strawberry blond curls pulled up in a bow at the side of her head and her hand in Peter's hand. Now, at Grandma's ninetieth, we handed great-grandchildren off from auntie to cousin and posed for countless more photos. Conversation was friendly, but superficial.

After filling his plate in the buffet line, Peter sat down at a table with several stiff, stone-faced old ladies from my mom's building and soon had them smiling. A half-hour later Mark hustled in from the airport in a golf shirt and khakis, looking a bit rumpled from the early morning flight. He scanned the room and made his way past the gray heads to his family, embracing each one of us but hugging Peter the longest because he lived the farthest away and we saw him least often.

After lunch everyone in turn raised toasts to my mom. Ann talked about the homemade pajamas that she got from Grandma nearly every year for Christmas. Lyn thanked Grandma for the inventive, colorful patches to her many pairs of jeans, which always provoked reactions in her dorm. Peter told of taking Grandma to buy a new television set, how she had researched the models, at age ninety, and how he had set the TV up and coached her on how to use the remote.

Before heading home, our family of five took pictures in the garden of Grandma's building. I had hoped to get the perfect image for our annual Christmas card photo. I'd add it to the five frames full of photos spanning twenty-five years which we always hung in the foyer during the holidays. One that day was perfect. There we were—the five of us lined up next to the pond on the garden wall, squinting in the sun and smiling, fresh faced, Minnesota nice. I was so proud of my family, so comfortable and complacent. I thought my family was perfect. I expected my joy to last forever.

We were together as a family for only fifteen hours. After Grandma's party, we relaxed at home with a movie. Mark unpacked his fishing gear while Lyn packed up her clean clothes. Peter set up his PlayStation, bragging a bit as usual about having purchased the hottest new toy on the market. The evening concluded—as had so many others over the years—with our huddling on the couch, newspapers strewn about the floor, snacks on our laps. I dozed off, and then slipped away to bed. I doubt I even said good night.

Lyn left at dawn to get back to camp before the arrival of new campers. Mark and I left for work, and Ann and Stephanie packed the car for their drive eastward to Stephanie's home in Long Island before they returned to school in Baltimore. Only Peter was home when Ann drove off. She said he hugged her and told her good-bye. Neither Ann nor Lyn saw Peter again.

F OR THE REMAINDER OF THE WEEK, Mark and I reveled in Peter's company. We worked but came home early to play golf. On our thirty-third wedding anniversary, July 3, we postponed our romantic date at a fine city restaurant in favor of burgers at a local grill with Peter.

One afternoon Mark helped Peter shop for a tent to use on upcoming cycling and camping trips Peter had planned with Mac, his flatmate in London. Peter tried on tents as though he were trying on shoes. "He must have climbed into ten or twelve of them," Mark told me later. "He rolled over and over, and his big feet kept sticking out the flaps. He had to find just the right size and shape."

The Fourth of July was warm and gorgeous, a bonus for Minnesotans who wanted to play on the lake. We started the day with a long bike ride. I usually had to work pretty hard to keep up with the two of them, Mark and Peter, but that day Peter stayed behind me. Churning as hard as I could up the biggest hill we had to climb, Peter said to me, "Go easy, Mom, let up on the gears. Shift down. You can do it."

Peter, always active, then went for a run. We would hear later that he had been talking about trying his first marathon. "Typical of Peter to go from one activity to another," we would hear. After his run, we ate sandwiches on the dock, and then went out in the boat. Peter stood behind his dad, urging him to go faster as he always did when he'd get bored with our cruising-to-see-the-new-houses routine. In the afternoon he and Mark golfed with another dad and son. The son would soon graduate from college with an economics degree like Peter's, and he wanted tips on how to get a similar job in investment banking. A few weeks later we would find that young man's resume on Peter's desk in London with several suggested contacts penciled at the top.

Todd came over to go water-skiing with Peter before fireworks. Mark drove the boat while I spotted. Both were beautiful water-skiers.

During their college summers, they used to ski early on calm mornings before work. Mark and I loved to watch them.

Once that week when Peter, Mark, and I were out in the boat together, I asked Peter about work and his social life. I didn't usually pry, but I sometimes worried he was working too hard, forgetting how to relax, or choosing work over fun like his dad had a tendency to do. He gently parried my inquiries. "This is just something I need to do right now. It won't last forever." He hinted at dreams of traveling to Australia, starting a business, or going to business school. He quickly rebuffed my questions about girls. "You're really worried about that, aren't you Mom?" He was only twenty-four years old. I don't know why I worried. I regret giving him the impression I was in a hurry for him to settle down into any sort of lasting relationship. He was still young.

Peter had always been discreet. Though his surface emotions were easy to read, he revealed little about his hopes and dreams, his anxieties, his fears. But moms weren't supposed to know too much about their twenty-four year old sons. Questions weren't welcomed.

Too soon we were at the airport to drop Peter off—Friday morning, July 6. Mark and I were both there, luckily, in one car because we were going out to dinner that evening to celebrate our anniversary. When we pulled up to the terminal doors, Peter hopped out of the car, put his bags down on the pavement, and hugged us both. I stood on the balls of my feet to take in the full effect. Then he swung his bags over his shoulders and pushed off with his laptop propped on his golf bag. I saw his big, broad charcoal-jacketed back go through the revolving door. He never turned around.

Peter flew to Philadelphia to meet his friend Pete Steinberg. Then the two of them drove to Atlantic City. The bachelor party was planned for Saturday night. We didn't hear from him again. I wish now I had called him the following day. I would have told him to be careful.

At dinner on Friday night Mark and I drank lots of wine. We often enjoyed wine with dinner, and excess hadn't been a problem. But the next morning, Mark, for the first time ever, commented about how much we had drunk. "We had way too much wine last night, Mary. We had no business driving home." Mark's statement was an uncanny omen of what was to happen to our son at the bachelor party that very night—in part because of the influence of alcohol.

Three

Week After

O
n the morning after the day our son had died, after a sleepless night, Mark and I sat numb and bleary-eyed at the kitchen table. This couldn't have happened. An effervescent eager young man, so full of promise, gone. I felt helpless, adrift, a tsunami barreling over me, tossing me, threatening to drown me. Surely the information was wrong. Wasn't there something we could do to rectify the situation? Change the outcome?

But already I sensed a terrible reality. I suspected we had reached a breaking point between life we knew and life as it would be forever after.

At eight, Mark's client and best friend, Will, came to take Mark for a bike ride, bringing me a café mocha. Spoonful by spoonful the whipped cream tasted delicious. Will brought us the morning papers and pointed out the article.

Man's N.J. death investigated: A man from Dellwood, Minn., died Sunday morning shortly after he was kicked out of a nightclub, according to the Atlantic County prosecutor's office. Peter Westra, 24, was . . .

I pushed it away. I couldn't bear to think of Peter as words in the newspaper.

. . . pronounced dead about 5 a.m. at the Atlantic City Medical Center. A friend of Westra's flagged down an Atlantic City police officer on

Peter at age twenty-one.

patrol at 4:17 a.m. and told the officer that Westra was hurt. Westra had been asked to leave the Naked City Nightclub on New York Avenue earlier. A call to the family home Sunday night went unanswered.—7-09-01

Will came the next day and the day after. The newspapers piled up on the corner of the table—the locals and the *New York Times.* While

Will and Mark biked, I walked. Though I'm a biker too, I felt too shaky. I questioned my balance. I was afraid I might get hit by a car coming out of a driveway. The phone started ringing early, people came, and I didn't want to miss anyone.

Our upstairs remodeling project stopped and the port-a-potty was hauled away from outside our front door. Friends hefted our queen-size bed back upstairs and set it up in Peter's room—already cleared out for painting, the carpet pulled away from the walls, photos and athletic ribbons and sailboat mobile packed up or given away—a shell of a room with no traces of the boy who used to inhabit it. Friends rearranged furniture, moved clothes racks, cleared the dining-room table of stuff that had been in our drawers, filled flower pots, repaired doors. The house became a blur of people. I had no idea how everyone thought of something to do, how it was decided who would water the pots on which days. I didn't care, I left details up to others.

For me, everything raveled out of control.

A 24-year-old investment banker from Dellwood whose death is under investigation by authorities in Atlantic City, N.J., was in the Twin Cities just last week to help celebrate his grandmother's 90th birthday. Peter Westra, who most recently worked in London, died early Sunday after being kicked out of an Atlantic City strip club where he attended a bachelor party with college buddies. "I'm dumbfounded this all happened," Westra's father, Mark Westra, said Monday. "I suspect foul play, but I don't know what happened."

. . . Charlie Zylstra, a spokeswoman for the family, said Westra was an avid outdoorsman who loved to canoe, bike and ski, and play golf with his father. "He was a wonderful young man, full of promise," she said. "He made friends wherever he went." Westra worked as an analyst in the real estate investment banking group at Deutsche Bank and was on temporary assignment for the bank in London. A bank spokesman said news of Westra's death stunned his co-workers. "It's a really hard time for the people who knew him," he said. "Everyone is very upset."

Calls to the Naked City were not returned Monday.—*Star Tribune*, 7-10-01

I spun a cocoon, shutting out the world, growing helpless and needy. Charlie, my best friend, a five-foot, two-inch bustle of love and concern, became manager of our fractured household, pattering from room to room, making tea, answering the phone, fending off reporters, taking care of my daughters. She set out a guestbook and greeted everyone who came to the door. She nurtured, soothed, and counseled. She knew before I did that the bedrock of my life had torn and its landscape would never be the same.

At dawn after our second sleepless night, Mark wanted to walk the golf course. He wanted to replay the last round he had enjoyed with Peter on the Fourth of July. Arm in arm, we walked the dew-coated fairways, holes one to eighteen. "Here's where Peter made the longest drive, a really good one, right down the middle of the fairway," Mark pointed out. "See that knob? From there he pitched right up to the cup." "His best putt here, it must have been thirty feet." Walking back to the clubhouse along the eighteenth fairway, I noticed the flag was flying at half-mast. I wondered why, and then it hit me. It was for Peter. Ah, this is big. Everyone must know. Suddenly, everything dropped completely from my grasp, and I sagged into Mark's shoulder.

> . . . Last October, the [Naked Lady] club faced losing its liquor license after police arrested four women on drug and prostitution charges following a month-long investigation. In August, the badly decomposed body of the club's doorman and cashier Charles Rhodes Campbell III was found behind a flooring company in Egg Harbor Township.
>
> In 1997, vice officers raided the club on the beach block of New York Avenue and charged one of the performers with prostitution. Proprietors Michael Morton and Ernest DiBono were charged with illegal alcohol sales and running a sexual-oriented business in violation of zoning laws.
>
> The club was closed Sunday evening. The neon red and purple sign with its busty-woman icon was turned off and a one-legged man sat talking to himself nearby.—*The Press of Atlantic City*, 7-09-01

In the evenings I retreated to the dock. It became my receiving station where I greeted visitors. When the bench grew full, I sat on the plank platform, watching my friends trundle down the hill, sober-faced, fighting tears. We told stories. We talked about Peter's spunk, his open friendliness, the impact of his too-short life. We didn't talk much about the homicide inquiry. We didn't know much anyway then. We were focused on how Peter had lived, not on how he had died, and I was grateful for that focus. Each evening at sunset, Bob and Be, old friends with whom we'd often traveled, came just to give me and Mark goodnight hugs.

As the homicide investigation continued, so did the phone calls. After one long afternoon on the phone with officials in Atlantic City, Mark said to me, "This is going to take years, Mary." He looked tired.

> . . . "Peter was just the best son a parent could ask for. He was a great boy, very generous, very kind. . . . We don't understand what happened," Mark Westra said. "It's bizarre. My son is not the kind of guy that gets into trouble. He's never been a problem-maker. . . . These are all good kids," [Westra said,] adding that his son's friends are young professionals in the banking, law and medical fields.—*The Press of Atlantic City*, 7-10-01

It was so unbelievably sordid. Kicked to death by bouncers outside a strip club. I was embarrassed, but I tried not to think about it. I could only guess what others, not our close friends, not the ones who came, might be thinking. Would they be saying: in the wrong place, at the wrong time, with the wrong words? They might be blaming Peter, or blaming us. I would learn that tended to happen with murder. For the moment I clung to the people in our inner circle. They buoyed our spirits and gave us courage.

P ETER'S ECONOMICS PROFESSOR AT MIDDLEBURY, Peter Mathews, was quoted in a news article in the middle of the week.

> . . . Last year, Westra co-wrote an article in the *Journal of Economics and Finance* on a new form of equity restructuring called a "tracking stock." . . . The paper had grown out of Westra's honor thesis and it received wide circulation through the Internet. It was a fantastic bit of research. Peter was a terrific young man. I think in many ways he was probably the quintessential Middlebury student. He was bright, he was energetic, he was engaging, he was ambitious, and he was athletic. John Elders . . . . Westra's adviser at Middlebury, said Westra had a well-earned reputation as a hard worker.—*Philadelphia Inquirer*, 7-10-01

Somehow we hobbled through the week. Over several days, we planned a memorial service. Whenever pastors Darlene or Linda came, and one or the other came every day, we gathered for a family conference in the quiet of our living room, away from the hubbub of the kitchen. Each day we planned a bit more, Linda deftly guiding us through the selection of hymns, the differences of opinion, the choice of eulogists, the differences of opinion, the violin soloists, and more differences of opinion. "You don't have to decide this today," she would say. "We can revisit it tomorrow."

During one family conference, from the middle of the sofa between the two girls, Mark said aloud, to no one in particular, "We can do this." I think he said it mostly for himself, but right then, in few words, he steeled our spines and set the tone for our family's survival.

Ann and Carolyn were present, but subtly absent. From the attic they hauled out the box labeled "Peter's Art Stuff" and began to arrange juvenile treasures on the dining-room table. Caught up in or maybe retreating from the throng of visitors, the girls were busy in other rooms with their own phone calls, their own friends. They probably didn't want to bother us, their parents, to upset us any more. It must have been excruciating for them to watch their mother and father navigate—and flail—in stormy waters. Lyn later called it "a painful blur . . . the house always full of people, an army of ladies making sure I ate. . . . Ann and I stay up all night, until three or four, or however long it took for our bodies to shut down so that sleep would come, and then we would sleep in a little in the morning, so that when we came downstairs the house was already full of people."

In the middle of one night, Mark and I heard raucous laughter rise through the two-story foyer from the dining room to the bed in Peter's room where we were lying awake. The girls and their friends were sifting through albums, selecting photos for the visitation and the memorial service. "This is such a dorky one. But we've got to put it in. It's Mom's favorite." By midday they had sixty photos ready to enlarge and mount on big black boards. They used silver marker to label the photos, and I can still find traces of it on the wood floor. I wouldn't buff them out for the world.

One evening, while we talked, our friend Pat crafted the obituary. When it appeared, I hardly recognized my son.

> . . . Peter was an enthusiastic golfer and cyclist who shared hours of recreation with his father and mother. He also enjoyed soccer, tennis, water-skiing, cross-country and downhill skiing. A 1995 graduate of Saint Paul Academy, he was a skillful athlete who contributed his best to the soccer team that won the state championship in 1994, the var-

sity cross-country ski team, and the varsity tennis team. Peter had a well-deserved reputation for being a hard worker. Whatever the playing field – his desk, the golf course, the ski track – he was a conscientious man who took on challenges with determination and good spirit. He set high goals for himself – and met them.

He was a catalyst for gathering friends. Outgoing, social, and endowed with a great sense of humor, Peter loved to get together with friends and bring new ones into his circle. Known to be thoughtful, giving, and respectful to all who knew him, Peter will be fondly remembered for his good nature, high values, and always apparent gratitude for the talents and blessings he was given. He was beloved by family, friends and colleagues in many cities and will be sorely missed.—*Star Tribune*, 7-11-01

I thought the obituary was too long, too laudatory. I wanted to remember his ugly big toes, his smelly socks, his little-boy pranks. I wanted Peter to look like flesh and blood, real, human, but I suppose we were in part trying to counteract the awful press, trying to make him more than the kid who went to a strip club and got drunk. "He was a pretty remarkable kid, you know," Mark said. I stopped the obituary the next day when the mortician told me the cost, not realizing Mark had intended for it to run for the remainder of the week, until Peter's friends arrived for the service.

Though we had not agreed on this decision or even discussed it, Mark and I tried hard to be together, with each other and with the girls, on every step of the difficult journey. We failed, of course, each of us in our own world, behind our own defenses, doing the best we could. Luckily our squabbles were minor: should the air-conditioning be on or off, the doors open or closed, the cat in or out.

Friends held us up, maybe even buffered our squabbles, during the day, but at night, alone, in our big bed in Peter's room, Mark and I were mush. We thrashed through too-vivid dreams. We lay numb, whispering and whimpering, holding each other until we heard the birds singing and the loons calling from across the lake. We refused all offers of medication—and there were many—for we were determined to feel, to remember, to suffer every pang. Only with dawn did I know I was awake, for I could no longer tell the difference between being awake and being asleep. I told myself that lying still was as restful as sleeping.

In the middle of the week when we were still in bed and bracing for the return of Peter's body, I told Mark I'd decided to give up alcohol. "I'm not making any promises to myself or to anyone else, and I'm not trying to set an example. I just don't want to take a chance on becoming dependent on alcohol." Too vividly I recalled the days after my sister's suicide when my father drank heavily, sobbing often and loudly, making scenes that garnered much sympathy while my mom bustled around the kitchen. For the remainder of my father's life, until he died at sixty-seven of cancer, his alcohol abuse caused rifts of concern in my family. I remembered how just a few nights earlier Mark and I had celebrated our anniversary with too much wine and drove home dangerously inebriated. "This is the time to play it safe. I want to honor my son. And I don't want to become a burden to my husband and my daughters. I must be present for my family." He hugged me and we wept some more.

We wrestled with whether or not to see Peter's body. I was afraid of what I might see—mangled limbs, dried blood, big bruises or dents, contorted face—something grotesque that wouldn't resemble the buoyant son I had seen a few days earlier, the son I wanted to remember. But Mark, Ann, and Carolyn were certain they wanted to see him, so we agreed to let the mortician advise us. Darlene, our pastor, who'd lost her own daughter, assured me that in time I would remember the living child rather than the dead body. "Seeing the empty body," she said, "can help in accepting the death."

On the short ride to the mortuary, sitting in the back seat of Will's car between my two daughters, I felt blinded by sunshine, as though I was emerging from a tunnel. Everything about White Bear Lake, where we'd lived for thirty years, looked familiar but cast in new colors, as it does sometimes after a long vacation.

Darlene was waiting at the door. I tiptoed into the solemn, dreary room. Everything was beige. I held my breath . . . there . . . a body lay on a table at the short end of a narrow long room. I moved closer. He was bare-shouldered with a drape tucked into his armpits. I approached the casket slowly . . . my hands over my mouth . . . quivering. My God, it was my son! He looked like himself . . . no make-up, no scrapes or cuts, only one big bruise on his right temple. His hair looked dull . . . Mark said later it might have been a wig. He looked exactly like the son I had seen only a few days earlier . . . but empty . . . not there. I touched him timidly. Or did I just wish I had? His skin was hard and cold. Or did I just imagine it so? Oh, how I wanted to pull back the drapes, check out his body, look for the birthmark on the side of his chest . . . but I know I didn't. I was afraid of finding slashes from the autopsy. I fixed my eyes on the hands . . . the huge hands, the long slender fingers, never any rings, the short clean nails. I wanted to hug him, kiss him . . . but I didn't. Instead I stared. I mumbled good-bye with a silent prayer. We huddled with Darlene in front of the table on which he lay and she blessed us all. Then we sat down by his body and stared some more. We each got up when we were ready, gave Peter a final good-bye, and exited the room. Lyn was last. She stood next to the table, looking at Peter for what felt like hours. Then she came out, dry-eyed, wordless. And we all went home . . . without Peter.

> A bouncer from Naked City strip club was arrested Wednesday and charged with murdering 24-year-old investment banker Peter Westra by repeatedly kicking him in the head after he was knocked to the ground outside the club. Westra, a Minnesota native who was at the South New York Avenue strip club for a friend's bachelor party, died of blunt-force trauma to the head and neck shortly after a confrontation with club employees Sunday.
>
> . . . Arrested was Egyptian native Tamer Shahid, 25, of the 1500 block of West Riverside Drive. He had been working at the club for about three weeks and has been in the country since July 1999.
>
> . . . Authorities described Shahid as just more that 6 feet tall, and weighing 225 pounds. He was wearing black leather, work-type boots at the time he inflicted kicks that killed Westra.—*The Press of Atlantic City*, 7-12-01

Even as I grew weaker physically, I felt stronger emotionally. It was as though I was outside of my body looking down on a woman trying to cope, trying to talk to people, floating on a wave of love and compassion in a very scary sea. Oddly, I didn't feel fragile. I felt empowered, strong, above the din and the horror. At one point, when a detail for the memorial service went out of control, I ranted so loudly, the girls rushed down from their rooms. Charlie put her arms around me. "Go ahead and scream, Mary. You have every right to scream."

I felt unpeeled, free to be totally myself, to bleed in front of everyone who came to the house. Every pore of my skin was stretched wide to absorb the slightest nuance in the air around the cocoon in which I was suspended. I couldn't follow group conversations, so I moved from group to group and sought out those who stood alone. I looked each person in the eye, listened, and hung on every word. I asked questions. When did you see Peter last? How did he look? What will you remember? I waxed cogent about loss, about faith, about death in the grander scheme of life. I thought I was making perfect sense; indeed, I felt as though I'd never been so intelligent or intelligible, never in my life had I connected so well with people.

It was like being high. I was high on the death of my son. I felt entitled to all the attention. Beaten and bruised myself, my privacy and my dignity shattered by events beyond my control, I had nothing to hide. Everyone read the sordid stories in the newspapers, yet these people knew

On the Isle of Wight in May 2001.

our son. I clung to my life-line—Peter had done nothing to provoke such a violent attack.

Within the shelter of my home, I was my rough, uncut self. My chest was ripped wide, my broken heart exposed and bleeding, blood dripping at my feet for everyone to see, everyone who dared to look. Why hide? Tears streamed down my cheeks.

I said what I wanted. I didn't give a rat's ass what anyone thought. If this had to happen to me, to Peter, and to our family, then I could say anything I wanted to these people who came to be near us. I felt obliged—even privileged—to be my most honest self.

I got a little crazy. During the tortuous half-sleeping, half-waking nights, I felt the presence of angels. I heard doors open and close. I heard loons calling, calling for me, I was certain. Soon I was flying with them over the lake, brushing the tops of the trees, looking for my beloved son. In the morning I splashed water on my face over and over again, slapping my skin, feeling exalted by the stimulation in each open pore, the ooze in each wrinkle. Even a simple bowel movement made me feel exquisitely alive.

Early morning, the day of the visitation, before I realized what was happening, Mark crawled on top of me. No cues, no foreplay, no words. Intense and urgent, without waiting for me to catch up, he was done in moments. It was an instinctual act of being human, a desperate affirmation of living, breathing, and being. Afterward, we clung to each other and wailed, not realizing then that we would cry for many months whenever we made love.

I didn't want to come out of the cocoon. I wanted shelter and protection. I was afraid to meet others, outsiders, those who had not ventured into the tight circle of the refuge of our home. What were they thinking? There must have been plenty of gossip about where Peter was, what he was doing, what he said, or about our being complicit somehow as parents. No matter what I told myself, my precious sense of dignity felt imperiled.

I was most afraid of the visitation. People would come and I wouldn't remember their names or faces. I wouldn't be gracious. I wouldn't have words. I was afraid I'd fall apart.

Dozens of people came whom I didn't immediately recognize, but everyone introduced themselves—Peter's teachers from preschool, the pastor who confirmed him, neighbors who had moved away, parents of

Peter's friends, and parents of the girls' friends. In an enormous outpouring of love, I felt totally embraced. We all did.

"Mary, don't you recognize me? It's me, Mac!" It was Peter's flatmate, whom I'd seen only six weeks earlier when we'd gone to London on the spur of the moment to visit Peter. But I wasn't expecting Middlebury kids until Friday. One of the Middlebury moms, a travel agent, had arranged a charter flight from New York for more than fifty classmates. But Mac came directly from London. We gave each other big hugs. "Come to our house, Mac." I wanted him close to us, and I wanted to give him the photo I'd framed of Peter and him at the finish of a race, the X-Adventure Ride, on the Isle of Wight in May.

Mark and I had watched the two of them compete in that event with Mac's mother, Petra, there from Chicago at the same time, conincidentally, whom we met when she emerged in rubber gloves after cleaning their bathroom—one task I would never undertake for any of my children. The boys assumed we'd go along with them to the Isle of Wight; Peter had already booked us into a B&B. So we followed the boys and their bikes onto the train. The race started early, so the boys left while we were still in bed. But after breakfast we rented bikes ourselves to try to find them on the course. We biked for miles without seeing them, then finally quit and waited on blankets at the finish. After five hours of mountain biking, canoeing, and running, Peter and Mac came in second to last, muddy and hungry—they had skipped breakfast—but ebullient over their effort. They stuffed themselves with food, pretty much constantly, the entire ferry ride back to the train.

After the visitation, our house was full of people. When I went upstairs to change my clothes, I found an eighteen-inch-tall cardboard cylinder someone had put behind the door in Peter's bedroom. It took me a moment to comprehend it was the box of Peter's ashes. It looked both too large and too small. I couldn't believe all of Peter's six-foot, three-inch body could fit in that cylinder.

Mark, Ann, Carolyn, and I took the cylinder of ashes out on the boat at dawn the next morning, Friday, July 13—the day of Peter's memorial service. Though several friends offered to help, Mark refused them all. "We can do this by ourselves," he said. He drove the boat to the middle of the lake and turned off the motor, so the boat bobbed gently in quiet waters while a curious loon swam near the bow. We took turns standing up, leaning over the side, scooping out handfuls of Peter's ashes, sprinkling them or flinging them into the water, giggling from time to time as the ashes dusted the sides of the boat in the breeze. The ashes seemed to last forever. A big body, we remembered. Then finally the cylinder was empty. "What are we going to do with it?" Ann asked. She filled it with water, capped it and dropped it in the lake, but it floated on the surface. "We can't just leave it," she said. Lyn suggested we go back to shore, get a big rock. So we picked a medium-sized one from the gravel near our dock and returned to the middle of the lake to drop the weighted cylinder into the water. This time it sunk. We brushed off the boat and our hands, started the motor, and took a couple turns around the lake, just for Peter.

"Faster, Mark, let's go faster for Peter," I said. "I want to feel Peter in my hair." I breathed deeply, basking in an exquisite calm as the wind ruffled my hair and bathed my face. It would be a long day.

Three more arrests in death at Atlantic City club. Police say others took part in beating of banker. The owner of Naked City strip club, its manager and another bouncer were arrested Thursday for their alleged roles in the beating death of 24-year-old investment banker Peter Westra.

Club owner Ernest DiBono, 53, of Absecon, manager Michael Charles Morton, 38, of Mays Landing, and bouncer Michael Dean Martinez, 45, of Atlantic City, were arrested at their homes and charged with participating in Westra's death by kicking the victim's legs and torso while he was on the ground.—*The Press of Atlantic City*, 7-13-01

. . . Lawyers for Mr. Shahid, Mr. DiBono and Mr. Morton said the men were not present during the beating. . . . Louis M. Barbone . . . said the bouncers tossed Mr. Westra from the club only after he repeatedly ignored warnings to stop groping the dancers. Even after Mr. Westra was outside, he tried to re-enter, Mr. Barbone said. "He was acting in a disorderly manner, especially concerning the dancers," he said. "There was concern by the dancers that he was basically stalking them inside the club." Mr. Blitz, the prosecutor, said he could not comment on suggestions that Mr. Westra was an unruly patron. "I'm focusing on what took place outside," he said. Some who knew Mr. Westra described him as a gentle, gregarious man who would never court violence. At 10 p.m. yesterday Naked City was open and the neon lighting that forms the silhouette of a woman on its façade was flashing There were no customers inside, and the half-dozen dancers sat at the bar talking. A simple flower arrangement and some ribbons had been tied to a parking meter in front of the club. On one of the ribbons, a former classmate from Middlebury had written, "In Memory of Pete."—*New York Times,* 7-14-01

Five arrests in five days, a symmetry that reassured me. On the day of Peter's memorial service, charges of assault, conspiracy of assault, and homicide were filed against five men. I felt glimmers of hope for a speedy, successful resolution, not realizing the process had barely begun.

That day lasted forever. I got dressed in stages over hours—first a shower, later my make-up, then the polar bear necklace that reminded me of Peter, and finally the black suit—telling myself at every step to be strong for the toughest and most public scene of my life. Only a few friends from out of town stopped by the house. Linda warned us the media might be present, but protocol was in place, she said. I shuddered at the prospect of thrill seekers at the memorial service for my son. I was seated in the Windsor chair by the front door, waiting for Bob to pick us up, when Mark came out of the guest room that was serving as our closet with two ties in his hand. "Which one of these ties of Peter's should I wear?"

I felt on view before the world. The only way I would get through this, I decided, was to pretend it was an obligatory performance. I was determined to be in control—tall, straight, strong. Friends who knew me would know it was just an act, that I was actually mush. I wore blinders as we were escorted into the church library. Our extended families hovered in the corners; I felt their eyes, but I couldn't look at them, or I'd fall apart. The four of us held hands in a circle. Darlene and Linda wrapped their arms around us, one of them whispering a prayer, as our families filed out of the room, past our lowered heads, into the sanctuary. Then Linda said, "Okay, follow me."

The longest walk of my life, single file behind Linda through the sanctuary to the far side to the first pew in front. From the corner of my eye I could see the entire church was full. Nearly a thousand people! I thanked God for the fullness of love and support for us, for Peter.

In my hands I clasped a photo of twenty-one year-old Peter, wearing a red tie, smiling at me, looking a little shy or uncommonly self-conscious.

Just like Linda said, we were carried away by the service.

Ruth, Mark's sister and closer to me than my own sisters, read from the lectern. "Peter Mark Westra was named with loving care after his paternal grandfather, Peter, and his father, Mark. In the Bible, Peter is called 'the rock' and Mark is considered his encourager and supporter."

His high school friend Todd said, "Whenever you were with Peter, he made you feel like you were someone special and very important to him."

His debate partner, Ellen, came forward with Kris, who'd been at camp when Lyn got the news, "Peter's friends were so important to him, sometimes he would forget that we didn't always know each other. Therefore parties at Peter's house were always interesting, sometimes awkward, with random groups of people interacting with one another. No matter how awkward the situation, it was always fun because Peter could make us laugh. He used to see how long he could keep us laughing. Eventually he just needed to stop because our stomachs hurt so badly."

Then Pete Steinberg walked forward from the middle of the sanctuary where he was sitting with his parents and his brother. The friend who was with our son when he died addressed his buddy before a crowd of people he hardly knew. "Peter, it has been the greatest pleasure of my life to be able to call you my friend. You know how many people you've touched, and how grateful they are to have known you, if even for only a short time. Wherever you are, I want you to know that I did everything I could to help you, and I know you'd have done the same for me."

Violin music floated from the balcony, mesmerizing me with a duet of Pachelbel's Canon, which Peter had played on a violin inherited from my father. It was as though the two of them were playing a concert now in heaven.

Then Linda eulogized a young man she did not know. "A unique, unrepeatable miracle of life and love and laughter. We are, and then we are not. Life has to be a mystery, because how short we would fall to try to come up with answers, especially when one has died a death as tragic and untimely as Peter's. This is not a time for answers; it is a time for questions, and a time for new resolve as we are in awe of how fragile life is, how simultaneously beautiful and dangerous life is. The promises of the God who gave his only son to a violent death."

She quoted Rev. William Sloane Coffin, giving us hope and an adamant refusal to blame God, to which we cling today. "When Rev. William Sloane Coffin's twenty-four year old son was killed in a car accident, he preached these words the following Sunday: 'The one thing that should never be said when someone dies is "It is the will of God." My own consolation lies in knowing that it was not the will of God that [my son] die. . . . God's heart was the first of all our hearts to break. . . . So I shall—so let us all—seek consolation in that love which never dies, and find peace in the dazzling grace that always is.'"

Darlene, who had lost a child herself, gave us a solemn sense of direction in her closing prayer. "Teach us to listen carefully for Peter's whispered encouragement in the days to come as he gently continues to assure his beloved family and all of us: 'You can do this. You can do this.'"

Can we? Can we do this? God, I hope so.

After the service, we stood like wooden soldiers at the far end of the parlor while a long line snaked around the room. Linda hovered nearby. "Unlock your knees. It'll be easier." Mark gripped my hand as he introduced me to business colleagues. So many faces, so many names. The girls' shoulders brushing mine, I felt pinned in place. Todd caught my eye from halfway across the room, while Charlie was whispering in his ear. Soon he sidled up to me. "Are you okay, Mrs. Westra? Just try to relax and enjoy these people." I breathed out, and my knees unlocked.

Suddenly I was confronted with a sea of black suits on young people looking overdressed for the hot July afternoon—Peter's Deutsche Bank colleagues from London and New York. One short young man clung to my hand. "I'm Bernard . . . from Paris." My mouth dropped—I didn't know Peter had been to Paris for work. I framed a question, but he moved on before I got anything out. Bernard and his colleagues departed that same evening, so we missed the opportunity to host them in our home. We would, however, see many of them in another month.

Mark nearly fainted, Charlie told me later, as he collapsed into Bob's car after the service. At home, the patio was crowded with family and out-of-town guests, some already bidding good-bye, by the time we returned. On her way out, the mother of one friend at the bachelor party, came up to me and took both my hands, tears filling her eyes. "I'm just so sorry that it was *your* son who was killed." I believed she meant that what happened to Peter could have happened to any one of the young men with him that night. She meant so well, but they were nice words that brought me small consolation.

Then dusk. A few of our closest neighborhood friends and several dozen young people clustered in corners of the patio. We served no alcohol—it would have been inappropriate since Peter had died in an alcohol-related event. And anyway, it wasn't a party. But as the hours passed, it sure felt like one. Ann and her friends on one side, Carolyn and hers on the other, Peter's friends in the middle. Peter would have loved the gathering. Typical of his parties, many of his friends were meeting each other for the first time. The stories began to roll as, one after another, the kids spoke up. Mark held court from his lounge chair in the middle, throwing his head back from time to time and laughing uproariously at tales we were hearing for the first time.

Steinberg made everybody laugh most. His younger brother Joe, among us on the patio, had visited the Middlebury campus as a prospective student. Peter and his friends wanted to show him a good time, so Peter invited Joe out, asking, "Joe, you want to have a good time? Tell them you're my brother." So Joe told everyone that evening he was Peter Westra's younger brother. Mark turned to Joe on the patio and asked, "And did you have a good time that night, Joe?" Bursting into a huge smile, he said, "Yeah, I had fun."

Another college friend, Jeff, told about meeting Peter for the first time on the green where Peter was playing croquet. Peter immediately asked Jeff to join the team. When Jeff asked how many other people were on the croquet team, Peter replied, "Just me." But soon Peter had gathered a team together and secured a grant from the college for professional-quality equipment. Peter had started, or restarted, croquet at Middlebury. He became the president of the croquet club and soon made it into a year-round sport.

Jeff also told us about Peter writing to the Schlitz brewing company, requesting T-shirts for their guys' intramural soccer team. He claimed they were poor college students who couldn't afford uniforms since they'd spent all their money on Schlitz beer. Jeff showed photos of the team, one in which they are bare-chested and another in which they all sport bright red Schlitz T-shirts. At that moment, several of the guys pulled back their oxford-cloth business shirts to show us red T-shirts they'd worn in Peter's honor to the memorial service.

Steinberg told about giving a tour for the admissions office one time when Peter planted one of their female friends among the visitors. Peter ran up to the group as they were walking through the campus, "captured" the five-foot, two-inch girl by throwing her over his shoulder, and carried her off to the nearby dorm and up the stairs to her room. The prospective students looked on, aghast.

By the end of the evening, we had a much fuller image of our twenty-four-year-old son, who had lived away from home since he was eighteen. He was more of a practical joker than we ever imagined. Yet sometimes it was a bit too much information. With one story about a German model in a hotel room, Ann stood up and bolted off, her entourage of friends following in her wake.

A neighbor had started a bonfire at the lakeshore, and many of us meandered down the hill. Blankets were spread and marshmallows offered. Everyone grew quiet and solemn. One by one, individuals approached me to tell me something about Peter, about times they had shared, about how they loved him.

Munir, who shared an apartment with Peter in Manhattan, told me how Peter had comforted him when his girlfriend was killed in an auto accident. He warned I might start doing weird things in my grief. He said, for example, he gave up eating meat, though meat was a mainstay in his culture. I told Munir, the first person I'd told other than Mark, about giving up alcohol. He understood immediately. "Would it be all right if I phoned you from time to time?" he asked me.

We'd never known our son to have a serious girlfriend. I had never seen him hold a girl's hand, but beautiful young women were in abundance that evening. One of the guys exclaimed, "I never knew Peter knew so many girls!"

I felt myself falling asleep on the blanket next to the fire. My watch read past midnight. Slowly I got up and made my way back up the hill, not wanting to fall asleep in the presence of visitors. I felt full and blessed. In one serendipitous moment, the truth hit me . . . just as I was passing the geraniums in my garden, the bonfire behind me, the house on the hillside ablaze in lights. I recalled some of the glowing words of the obituary: "conscientious, endowed, thoughtful." Yes, I admitted to myself, those words were really true. Peter was a remarkable young man. And if he was remarkable, then I must have been a pretty good mom. I could take some credit for raising him.

The party continued all weekend, young people coming and going with swimsuits and motel towels, neighbors stopping by on their boats, Ann taking her friends waterskiing in our boat, Lyn tubing with her friends in another. The next evening a barbecue materialized when neighbors helped out, another late-night bonfire. On Sunday afternoon about twenty friends returned for a final good-bye on their way to the airport. Mark and the guys sat in one room of the house, the girls and I in another. I felt like the wise old mom as they asked questions about what Peter was like as a baby and in elementary school, whether or not I had worked, what it was like to be his mother. And they shared dreams and aspirations with me and told me about their moms. Several said they would be going home soon to touch base in the wake of our tragedy. They promised to send more photos, more stories, and they assured us they would stay close through the trial.

"We will be eager to see you anytime, anyplace," we told them. From that day, Peter's friends became a safety harness of love and support for us, a connection to Peter and to the man he would have become. We loved them . . . because he loved them.

Four

First Month

I felt forever changed. An uncomfortable silence hung over our home, over our future, in the still days and weeks after the memorial service. The dock became the gravesite where I could talk with Peter, next to the gulping water into which we had committed his ashes.

I spent idle hours on the lounge chair on the dock, soaking up the balm of the sun, throwing big questions to the lake and the sky: Where are you now Peter? Do you see us? What are we supposed to make of this tragedy? My life in paradise felt over, done with, gone, and I had never realized how good I had it.

Murder was a word I simply could not grasp—a statistic or a story line in television or the movies, not something that happened to good people, not in this neighborhood, not to conscientious, tax-paying parents who had worked long hours for every one of the comforts they were heartily enjoying.

I HAD NEVER EXPECTED TO BECOME a stay-at-home mom. When Ann was born a month before my thirtieth birthday, I had intended to take only a short leave before returning to teach high school English. But after spending a couple months with my adoring infant, I was smitten. Mark was working long hours as a new attorney. I told myself I was making things easier by staying at home, and he agreed. We were new then to White Bear Lake, having moved back a few months earlier from the Bay Area, where Mark was in the Navy and after his service attended law school while I taught French. We had gotten married six years earlier right after his college graduation, just before he'd joined the officer corps to avoid being drafted and sent to Vietnam. I went with him to Newport, Rhode Island, Athens, Georgia, and finally Oakland. We used to joke that as soon as we'd drive into town, he'd stop at the local school board, and I'd have a teaching contract in hand before we even rented an apartment.

I didn't really want to move back to Minnesota. Though I had grown up in Minneapolis and met Mark at college in St. Paul, returning to my home state felt like a move backward, too close to my family. But Mark got a good job offer from a prominent St. Paul firm. So we bought an old farm house in White Bear Township, a half hour from my parents, and started what would be ten years of fix-up projects. We knocked out plaster and lath, burned the lath in the living room fireplace, and buried

Peter's first steps.

plaster in the yard where there'd once been a chicken coop. On weekends Mark reroofed and rewired using knowledge he had gained from manuals. And I became Total Mom—my first circle of friends were La Leche League moms who breast-fed toddlers and even preschoolers. I canned tomatoes and made casseroles and baked cookies while almost always, it seemed, a child of mine sat on the counter and snitched dough.

Ann was twenty-one months old and still nursing when Peter was born in February of 1977. Though Ann's birth by midwife was uneventful and we had gone home then after only one night in the hospital, Peter's birth kept me there two nights. My waters had broken late in the evening while Mark was at dinner with clients, just as his appetizer arrived, he likes to remind me. He came home and took me to the hospital, but nothing happened. We waited until late the next morning for the nurses to start a pitocin drip and soon Peter came in a rush: big, strong, and docile. We named him after his paternal grandfather, Peter Westra, a Presbyterian minister who had married Mark and me nine years earlier. At eight pounds, five-and-one-quarter ounces, and twenty-and-a-half inches, Peter was the lightest of my three babies, but at five months he weighed twenty pounds, a bald and perfect chunk.

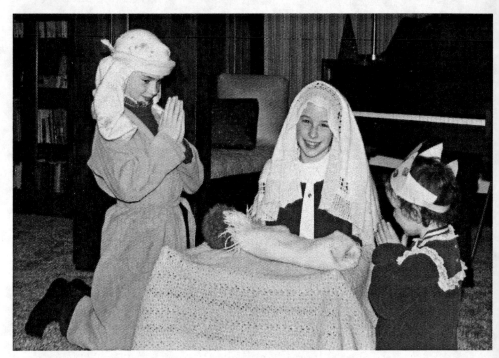

Peter, Ann, and Carolyn playing the Nativity.

I HAULED MY KIDS EVERYWHERE. Convinced no one would recognize me if I didn't have them in tow, we shopped ensemble, toddler in one hand and baby on the hip, or two kids in a grocery cart with little room for toilet paper. At home, we worked—me scrubbing the bathroom floor with Ann "helping" while Peter sat in his infant seat; she turning the waste basket over his head, "kissing" him, and leaving bite marks on his forehead.

We never worried about spoiling our babies. We picked them up whenever they cried. We espoused the family bed. When they stopped nursing as toddlers, Mark read aloud to them on their beds until they fell asleep. Mark still chides Ann, now a pediatrician, about how she never fell asleep alone in her bed until she was in kindergarten.

Even as a kid, Peter had energy. Sometimes I'd shop with him during Ann's preschool mornings. I remember his climbing into a store window and attacking the furry coats as though they were beasts and then hiding under the clothes racks. He could sit still too, at home, making cars and trucks out of play dough at the kitchen table, and he could focus for hours, setting up castles of Legos on the floor or making houses out of big boxes. But he most adored drama. When the little girl next door came over to play, Peter dressed as "dad" in overhauls or as the "groom" in his dad's old jacket and a tie that hung to his knees. In one photo he's robed as Joseph while Ann tends to the baby Jesus in her doll's cradle. His baby book, ironically the most complete of the three baby books I kept, detailed the action: *Ann seems to have all the ideas, but you have all the nerve.*

One Saturday morning when Ann was two and a half and Peter just nine months, we were getting ready to paint the spare bedroom. Mark had lined up the painting supplies on the landing of the stairs outside the room and I was in the kitchen waiting for the sitter. Suddenly a partially opened can of white latex paint came tumbling down the carpeted stairs, and Peter came tumbling after it—coated from bald head to big toe in white paint. We doused him with soap and water and rinsed his eyes after talking to the doctor but averted, that time, a trip to the emergency room. We'd return later for a broken arm.

What were we striving for then? What were our goals? What did I want?

I asked myself all those big questions from my perch on the dock. Just the best for our kids, like everyone else. Yes, we hoped for a nice house in a good community. But mostly we just wanted a green and leafy environment in which to raise our family.

It wasn't about safety. Safety was something we took for granted. Yet soon after we moved a mile and a half away to our house on the lake, when Ann was ten, Peter, eight, and Carolyn four, I saw little lights flashing in the backyard and worried someone might be staking us out. The cop scoffed. "Lady, this isn't a high crime area." The lights probably came from fireflies, we decided.

Carolyn was born a month before Peter turned four. Together Peter and I took the new baby to Ann's kindergarten for show-and-tell, cuddled for naps on the double bed in his room after my C-section, and prepared meals in matching aprons while Carolyn dozed in her car seat. But I worried he perhaps didn't get enough mothering, or his share of nurturing, for he always had a strong sense of fair play, right and wrong.

"One time when a clown visited school," wrote a preschool teacher after his death, "the clown decided to face paint three or four children. Peter wasn't in the group the clown had time to do and his sense of preschool injustice was roused. In other words, he was upset!"

He didn't like people to butt in lines in front of us. He chided me when I was curt to the clerks at convenience stores. Though I wouldn't exactly call him demanding, I think he struggled for his equal share of attention.

In his baby book, I recorded his preschool words: *When you were mad at me, you said, "Mom, I not like you and I not love you and you're not pretty." You called me, "Dummy, lummy, bummy Mom."*

Peter got attention by being active, precocious, engaging. He chattered incessantly even when his mangled *th*'s and *b*'s made him difficult to understand. Speech therapy in elementary school helped him overcome speech impediments, but even as an adult he'd be accused of mumbling, a trait he shared with his father.

I tried to remember each stage . . . playing run-around-the-dining-room-table with toddlers in pj's, advancing to hide-and-seek in the dark with flashlights, driving Big Wheels in the driveway, diving into leaf piles, dressing snowmen in the front yard, riding our bikes to Cup & Cone, Peter riding his bike into the rear end of a parked car.

Carolyn was born four years after Peter. She learned early how to get a rise out of her big brother. She upset his castles, got into his baseball

Peter, ten, and Carolyn, six.

collection, stole his magazines. I probably protected my younger child, but Peter often had unrealistic expectations for her behavior. He seemed to think she should act *his age*. How sweet it was for all of us when he finally, sometime in junior high, realized he only had to be nice to her and she would worship the ground on which he walked. He eventually totally won her over. Peter got his bookish younger sister to join the swim team in summer, the cross-country ski team in winter. They took violin lessons together and played duets. Lyn told me, "Peter always had big plans for me."

Hands down, Peter's favorite buddy was his dad. As soon as the little boy heard the honk of Mark's car in the driveway at the end of the day, he'd rush to the door. On Peter's fourth birthday, Mark wrote in his baby book: *He is very much Dad's boy. When he doesn't wake up before I leave for work, he is quite unhappy. He even asks that I "sit" on him in the morning to wake him up, but often to no avail. Peter is my helper with many projects until he loses interest or until his chatter causes me to totally lose my concentration.*

On weekends Mark and Peter dressed in matching bib overhauls to plant the garden or, with both of them wearing tool belts, to work around the house. In the evenings they wrestled on the floor, even once Peter got quite big. They played pickup hockey together in the park on Sunday afternoons. When Peter was in junior high and started to focus on soccer, they set up a goal post in our backyard. I still hear Peter calling, "Dad, let's go kick around the soccer ball." Peter talked his dad into taking scuba lessons. He signed them both up for the Ironman, a bike ride near the Twin Cities that they did for five straight years. Peter encouraged his dad to cross-country ski. One summer after college he brought home two lacrosse sticks. "Dad, let's go play lacrosse."

Peter had a knack for motivating people.

Our solid, two-story stucco home sits on a broad, triangularly shaped lot at the cusp of a little hill in old Dellwood, a small community of only one thousand, regarded as extremely private, tucked between lakeshore and farmlands. I can bike two miles and be at an apple orchard; another mile and I'm among cows.

Our eighty-year-old home was originally a summer home, one of several along this stretch of shoreline built by wealthy Saint Paul families, who came by streetcar to avoid the summer heat and disease in the city. We were the first family to live year-round in our house. Its wide grassy lawn at the street narrows to only thirty feet of lakeshore, just enough for a dock and a boat. The south side of the house is mostly windows, all double-glazed now, overlooking the lake. We've added furnaces, repainted, and redecorated. No one would ever guess this used to be only a summer house.

As the second-born, Peter chose his room after Ann, and he did not get a lake view. But he got the larger room with its own bath. I remember his eighth birthday party in that room, before we moved in, eight little boys in camouflage clothes sitting around a plastic map on the floor, playing with action figures, and then getting up to bowl the length of the empty room.

Of course, we had our challenges. I remember going out in the boat after church one day to check how Ann and Peter were doing in a multi-class sailing regatta. It was a windy day and there were many boats rounding the buoy, but Fast Eddie, the boat we had leased from the yacht club, was nowhere among them. Peter had steered way off course and was just trying to get back to the dock without more trouble, because he had collided with an M-16 in an earlier leg, clipped the side stay of that boat, and caused its mast to fall. The seasoned sailor who owned the M-16 told Mark later that he hadn't really yelled at Peter, that such accidents do happen in busy regattas, but the deed was done, and Peter was mortified. He never wanted to sail again.

When Peter was in ninth grade, Nordic skiing was just becoming a viable varsity sport. He skied with a couple older guys, recruited younger skiers, and by his junior year had helped to build a team of which he was, of course, one of the captains. A math teacher who has become our friend told the story of Peter talking her into becoming the coach. "We won't be able to have a school team, Mrs. Scott, unless you coach us." Sixteen years later, she's still coaching. She has initiated a Nordic skiing event, the annual Peter Westra Sprints, for local high school skiers, at which she wears a photo of Peter's championship medley team on a ribbon around her neck.

In junior high the girls called often. "Is Peter there?" But it seemed like he'd mumble a few words and hang up quickly. He soon lost his braces and his freckles, grew taller than most of boys, worked out, and got muscular. He was a pretty handsome teenager, if a mom might say so, with a square chin, biggish ears, dark brown hair, and an oversized Adam's apple. He was by no means the school stud, but he was outgoing and smart. Everybody—teachers, coaches, kids and kids' parents—liked him.

In tenth grade, he became pals with many of Ann's classmates, even though they were two grades ahead of him. He knew them from varsity sports and the debate team. When one of Ann's friends asked him to the senior prom, Ann was unhappy: Peter was encroaching on her space.

When her friends came to the house, they sought Peter. It didn't help the situation when he took out the riding lawn mower and gave the city kids rides around our yard.

ANN BECAME THE DESIGNATED DRIVER as soon as she turned sixteen. In the sturdy used silver Volvo we got to serve as our third family car, she took her brother to school and waited for him after school and sports activities. It didn't always work well.

Late one Friday night after a school event, she came into the house alone.

"Where's Peter?" Mark asked.

"He was being a jerk," she replied.

"Where is he, Ann?"

"I don't know. He made me mad. I waited for him forever, and then he fought me over the radio station. I get to choose! I'm the driver."

"Ann, what did you do with Peter?" Mark implored, his voice rising in anxiety.

"I made him get out of the car. He's somewhere by the freeway and Pennsylvania Avenue. I stopped the car and he got out. So I drove off. I guess he's there."

We couldn't believe it. She had left her fourteen-year-old brother at ten-thirty at night in a sketchy neighborhood fifteen miles from our home. Mark was furious. He grounded her for two weeks and left immediately to try to find him. Driving slowly up and dark darkened streets, stopping and calling for him, Mark finally saw Peter emerge, truly shaking, from the shadows of a building. I doubt Peter called his sister's bluff again.

We knew he could be stubborn. He wanted to be his own person, not the younger brother of his over-achieving older sister. While Ann would lay out chits of paper on her bed in order to memorize details for the next day's test, Peter would be asleep by nine-thirty. For him, an A- on his report card was generally good enough, though he'd get frustrated if he misjudged his progress and wound up with a B+. He had his own goals. His best subject was math, yet that was the class in which he received his lowest grade because he didn't like the teacher. Still, he got a perfect 800 on his math SATs.

Once when he was in eleventh grade, we were called to school because Peter had gotten into a fight. Details were sketchy, but we heard

Ann, sixteen, and Peter, fourteen, leaving for school.

Peter had been teased by a classmate while he was selling roses for Valentine's Day as part of a class committee. We heard that the other boy might have tried to take one of the roses without paying for it. Anyway, punches were exchanged, and both were suspended for a couple days.

After Peter's death, his high school advisor, who was also the French teacher and dean of students, wrote us a note. She had learned of his death while attending a conference on integrity and ethical education in Santa Fe. "It was a perfect context in which to grieve and to reflect on Peter's life, as he was one of the most ethical young people I know. He always took the time to discern right and wrong, to act on it, and to articulate why he had made his choice."

She went on to write: "One February afternoon of his senior year, Peter appeared in my office with the characteristic twinkle in his eyes and grin on his face. He thought we needed a "snow day", as there had been very few during his high school career and time was running out. He didn't believe that, as dean of students, I did not have the school code to cancel school on radio. He suggested that we could probably figure it out if we tried hard enough. Peter and I spent part of that afternoon phoning the station and "trying" various obvious codes. We used the school address, the first several digits of the phone number, and even spelled out "snow" on the phone keypad—no luck! To this day, I don't remember what numbers we used but, all of a sudden, we were transferred to the cancellation desk. We both giggled—and then quickly hung up!!"

PETER LOOKED LIKE A LEADER. With his height, he was easily noticed. But he smiled, engaged others in conversation, and tried to be liked. He had a good sense of humor. He didn't lord authority over others. He learned when to stay back and went along with the crowd, but only to a certain extent. When his soccer team beat Apple Valley, the state champs, the boys on his team got their ears pierced. Peter wore the metal stud a bit self-consciously, and I managed to not over-react. Then it was decided that if the team took the state high school championship that year, they'd get tattoos. The team lost to Apple Valley in the quarterfinals, took the earrings out, and didn't get tattoos.

Not that he didn't have flair. Pictures of Peter show his hair in cornrows when his Nordic ski team took third place in the state medley competition. More pictures show him in old-fashioned wool knickers and knee socks for ski races. One picture shows him and his buddy Kris dressed for a ski meet in only long underwear and boxer shorts, with the image of an elephant's trunk stuck in a strategic spot.

Oh, those photographs. The images are so firmly ingrained in my mind. I can conjure them up even without reopening the albums.

One of his junior high soccer teammates reminded us of the match in which the goalpost came crashing down on our goalie. Most of the guys stood there waiting for the referee, but Peter went running up the field and began lifting the goal post off his teammate, instinctively knowing what to do while the others seemed stunned. He was always so earnest.

I didn't always appreciate his energy, it pains me to admit. I was overly concerned about his messy room and dirty sweaty socks. I yelled at him to get up and get going in the morning, doing what I thought was important. I yelled too much, I'm sure, and I was too much in his face when he came home after sports, exhausted and hungry. I remember telling him not to snack, to wait for dinner, and his retort, "Mom, it will not ruin my appetite!"

Peter had his own ideas of how to do things, and he never hesitated to tell me. I remember the exact moment—he was probably twelve—when his eyes no longer met mine, and he was taller, and therefore more powerful, than I. That was the moment I knew I needed to develop other strategies.

But still I ranted. Peter made me angry. I was not the all-calm parent. I wish I had done many things differently.

One time, when he was sixteen, I was on an early evening bike ride with girlfriends. We were pedaling on a dirt road through a golf course about ten miles from home, and I was complaining loudly to the others about my loutish teenaged son. Suddenly, I heard a deep voice rising from the golf green that was tucked behind the trees. "Hi Mom!" Peter yelled. I nearly toppled over. Peter was golfing with friends and had heard my voice, but luckily he hadn't picked up on my words.

I wish I could take back those words.

Mark and I drove Peter to Middlebury College in August of 1995. Our jeep packed to the max, two bikes and a rocket box full of skis on top, we stopped in Chicago for a Monet exhibition, and then paused again at Fort Ticonderoga on the shores of Lake Champlain, before crossing into Vermont. We got Peter settled into his room and met a few of his dorm mates on the ground floor, among which three were named Peter. They immediately devised a system to differentiate the Peters. One was called Sushi Pete, one was Nerdy Pete (that was Peter Steinberg), and, for a while, our Peter adopted the nickname "Stra."

It was Mark who was sad on our drive back to Minnesota. When we stopped at the Wisconsin border to buy a few groceries, Mark, who had begun doing the family grocery shopping when I returned to work, broke down in tears. "It's just not going to be so fun to shop anymore without Peter there to eat the food."

Peter intended to play varsity soccer and to cross-country ski at Middlebury, but by his sophomore year he had given both up for several intramural soccer teams—male and coed—as well as hockey, croquet and investment club.

He tried to learn Japanese. We heard about his wearing a headset around campus while practicing pronunciation. Math remained his best subject, and soon he was an economics major with a computer science minor. A friend wrote: "I remember doing economic problem sets with Peter and watching him look at a complex math word problem and simply write down the answer. I would say, 'What is that you just wrote?' Peter would retort, 'The answer.' And after explaining the problem to me through line-by-line equations, we would end up with just that, the answer Peter had written down."

Nobody said he studied all the time, though he stayed on the dean's list. He had fun and was the butt of as many jokes as he perpetrated. A classmate wrote: "There were maybe twelve sophomore boys, not a single woman, waiting for our computer science class to begin . . . taught by the lovely AB. We all harbored a certain affection for the lovely professor B, but this fateful day Pete made the unfortunate decision of admitting that he did indeed have a crush on her. We immediately started in hazing Peter about it. He turned bright red and jumped up when he thought he heard Professor B coming down the stairs. He pulled his meanest face out of his bag of tricks and put it on, "Okay. You guys better stop before she gets here." The poor bastard didn't even realize that was just fire for the flames. The class was in hysterics and Peter was the color of a cherry tomato by the time B entered the room. I've never heard a silence so complete as when she asked, "Hey guys, what's so funny?" The silence stretched on for a few more eternal seconds until another classmate answered, "Peter farted . . . really loud."

We talked regularly while he was away at college. We heard about his activities, we listened, and we tried not to ask too many questions. We went each fall to parents' weekend, where invariably Peter would arrange dinner at a local restaurant with us and several of his friends. For New Year's Eves, on break from college, he entertained his high school friends in our home with what he decided would be a formal party—dress shirts and ties and dresses. In preparation, he pulled out recipe books, purchased the ingredients, baked hors d'oeuvres, and made fancy mixed drinks in the blender. In the morning Mark and I made pancakes for those friends who remained under blankets on our family-room floor.

Peter was a doer, not a talker. One college buddy wrote, "As I look back I wish I had dug deeper and asked more questions. That was just not Pete. I think he was more interested in you."

His friends called him the ultimate wing man ready to do anything, quick to laugh, eager to make others feel comfortable. After college, on his forays back to New York City from London, apparently word would spread quickly by cell phone: "Westra's in town! Let's get together!"

AFTER GRADUATION FROM MIDDLEBURY Peter went to work as a financial analyst in Manhattan for Deutsche Bank. He found an apartment two blocks from the World Trade Center, a two-bedroom converted to three that he shared with two Midd classmates.

I'll never forget the day in late June of 1999 when my two oldest children fledged the nest on the same sunny morning, Peter for his job in New York and Ann for a year in San Francisco before she started medical school. Their styles of departure exemplified the contrast in their personalities. A couple high school girlfriends and Todd waved Peter off at six in the morning, when he climbed into the cab of a huge Ryder truck, drove down our driveway, and turned east. Ann packed up her white Jetta, alone, and turned west. She called later that afternoon to say she'd gotten tired and had checked into a motel in western South Dakota, but we didn't hear from Peter until the following afternoon. He had driven all night, finally pulled into a rest stop in Ohio, opened the rear door of the truck, and slept on our old couch.

I wish I had told him how beautiful he was.

On his first Thanksgiving weekend working in Manhattan, we met him and Lyn, who came down from her freshman year of college in Maine, in New York City. I waited for Peter at the restaurant he had reserved while Mark waited at our hotel for Lyn, for we were going to the theatre after dinner. I can see Peter stepping out of the cab, gorgeous, coming straight from the airport because he had just flown in from business in London. He was wearing a new ankle-length black wool coat with a beautiful long white scarf hanging under the collar. Unabashedly proud, he stroked it lightly. "Pretty nice, huh Mom?"

The next day we stood in the rain near Grand Central Station for Macy's Thanksgiving Day parade. Peter brought donuts and stood behind

Peter, twenty-two, leaving for New York City.

us, so tall he could see over us. He took us to the Mesa Grille near Union Square for a Thanksgiving dinner with a southwestern twist, and then to a James Bond movie. We were challenged to keep up with his big steps as he led us through Washington Square, around corners, up stairs. On Saturday we walked from his apartment to Battery Park to board the ferry to Ellis Island. He and Lyn mugged for the camera in front of the Statue of Liberty. Then afterward we bought deli sandwiches near his office and settled on benches for a picnic on the World Trade Center Plaza, content to be there since the line for the elevator to the restaurant Windows on the World was too long.

On Sunday morning, after Lyn had boarded the train and before we left for the airport, we arranged to meet Peter a final time at the corner of Spring and Mercer in Soho. We looked all over for him. We got on our cell phone to locate him. "Don't you see me?" he asked. "I'm right across the street from you." There he was—athletic shorts, T-shirt, baseball cap turned backward, on Rollerblades! But I can't forget the long black coat and white scarf: a sophisticated man of the world one day and the next, the kid who used to live with us.

I wish I had told him how well he entertained us.

Five

More Months

It was little more than a month since Peter's death. I kept thinking he was just asleep across the ocean. That's why we weren't hearing from him.

Charlie, in town from Yankton, stood with me in the driveway when the moving van pulled up to the house. Two young men got out of the truck and began to unload box after box and to arrange them in the garage. They stacked three thin rectangular boxes of bikes against the wall. I got more and more nervous as I watched the delivery boys work. I couldn't stop myself from blurting out the story of what had happened to Peter. "Be careful," I told them, "when you're out with your friends." The movers hardly glanced my way.

As soon as the van drove off, I began to paw through Peter's boxes. I found shirts and sweatshirts on hangers, athletic bags, shoes in layers of cream-colored packing paper, and I told Charlie, "I need to be alone for a while."

I chose the size fourteen Bally loafer I'd seen him wear so often. I pulled out the black leather belt, almost new and not much wider than my own waist. I grabbed my journal and the photo album the girls had assembled for the services and headed down to the dock to spend some time with Peter. I sniffed his shoe. I fingered his belt. These things that had so recently touched his body held little scent. I turned the pages of the photo album through a veil of tears, working my way backward from the day Peter had worn these same shoes and this same belt at my mom's ninetieth birthday party. I couldn't believe I wouldn't see him again.

What did I have of him now, I asked in my journal. His new-comer's guide to New York City. The pricey mountain bike he had purchased for the X-Adventure Ride on the Isle of Wight. Two pairs of skis with his name on them in the excellent condition in which he maintained his gear. Boxes of sweaters and T-shirts and fleece and athletic shoes and shin guards. Button-down shirts of every color, jeans, cords, a few barely worn pants. Body-hugging shirts in the "European" style one of his female friends had helped him select on a shopping foray but that didn't quite suit his broad American build. Ten boxes in all—a career—leisure—boxes of books and files and tools—relationships—his personhood and his livelihood—his happiness—his realm—his life.

I gazed at the photos and thought about what I'd never lose. His smile—so full and bright, changing from the grimace of his younger years, teeth astray, to a big bold honest smile. His eyes—dark and twinkling, looking directly at the photographer, big dorky glasses on the kid, contact lenses in high school, and then wire rims in college that he thought made him look sophisticated. Bushy, dark eyebrows, tufty at the center. Full lips. Muscular frame—broad shoulders, always in shape. His laugh—how I yearned to hear it again! The feel of his big hand on my shoulder, saying, "It's okay, Mom." The hair on his chest, not quite that of a full-grown man's, but definitely getting there. The birthmark on the side of his chest under his arm. And marvelous hair that looked great in any style, hair I loved long and wavy but that he preferred short like George Clooney's, hair that at age twenty-four already had patches of gray on the sides just behind his ears. We chided him about those gray patches, but he was proud of them.

I was determined to hang onto the little things. I wanted to feel each and every one of them—the big shoe at my chest, the soft leather belt and chilly clasp in my fingers, the ripple on the water, the glow of the sunshine, the call of the loon, the jump of the fish, the glint of the moonlight, the magic of the falling meteor, the rustle of the breeze in the trees, the soft wind on my face, the warm tears on my cheeks. Every photo, every experience, every image, sighs, gasps, space, emptiness, loneliness, and love.

W E WENT TO NEW HAMPSHIRE for the wedding of the young man whom Peter and his friends had feted in Atlantic City. Brad and his parents had urged us to attend, in Peter's place, when they came to Minnesota for the memorial service. Mark was hesitant, but I wanted to seize every occasion to stay in touch with Peter's friends, and I thought we could mourn and celebrate at the same time. I was wrong, however. The wedding was painful, and I'm sure our presence detracted from everyone else's joy. My tears flowed as soon as the group gathered for photos around the Middlebury banner, and I bolted totally when the groom danced with his mother. We should not have gone to that wedding.

We also attended a memorial service for Peter on Fifth Avenue in Manhattan sponsored by Deutsche Bank and Middlebury College. Ann came from Baltimore, Charlie and Bob from Yankton, along with a couple dozen Middlebury friends and nearly a hundred of Peter's work colleagues. More stories delighted and comforted us. One colleague told us Peter kept a soccer ball under his desk and pulled it out for play when he worked on Saturday mornings and working moms brought their young kids into the office. I can hear him say, "Hey, wanna kick this around with me?" Pete Steinberg and Mark's friend Will repeated the eulogies they'd given in Minnesota, and then Peter's boss spoke. "My son is only seven years old, but I can only hope one day he becomes half the man that Peter Westra was."

Then we flew to London for another Deutsche Bank service, toting again the big photo boards the girls had arranged. On the flight I listed questions I hoped to ask his colleagues: What did he wear to the office? What was his typical day like? Did he eat at his desk? Did he talk about his home? Could you tell when he was irritated or tired? Who were his mentors? I was hungry to learn as much as I could about a son who had grown up away from home and become an adult while I wasn't watching.

That afternoon, the cozy, war-scarred, three-hundred-year-old Anglican chapel, St. Botolph's-Without-Bishops-Gate, sitting in a patch of garden surrounded by tall buildings near Liverpool station, held a couple dozen of Peter's colleagues from his nearby office and even more Middlebury friends. Mac, Peter's flat-mate, told of their plans for future hiking and biking trips and hinted at the time they had recently skated through the British Museum to verify the security they'd seen in *The Thomas Crown Affair*.

The vicar's final words soothed my pain and left me with images that would continue to comfort me when I sat on my mourning bench at the dock and stared into the heavens. "And Life is eternal and Love is immortal, and death is only a horizon, and a horizon is nothing, save the limit of our sight. Lift us up, strong Son of God, that we may see further. Cleanse our eyes that we may see more clearly. Draw us closer to Thyself, that we may know ourselves to be nearer our loved ones who are with Thee."

I felt a flicker, just a flicker, of accepting his death during that memorial service. Maybe because he still felt so alive. I felt the hope, if not the presence, of peace. I would continue to embrace the image of the horizon: not gone, just out of my line of vision, behind the trees on the other side of the lake, near me.

Afterward, at the Two Cows pub down the street, a place Peter and his mates had frequented after work, the stories flowed as freely as the pints. Everyone had a story about how much he or she loved our son, how genuine he was, how he really listened when they talked to him. We heard about a recent ski weekend at the boss's villa in Switzerland when Peter chose to spend the first day with the beginning skiers, though it was clear his skill level was advanced. Someone mentioned his grace on skis, how amazing it was, considering Peter's height and high center of gravity.

That evening Elaine, another of Peter's colleagues, hurried into the pub just we were saying good-byes. Elaine hadn't been able to get away from work for the memorial service, but she wanted to see us. She wanted to tell us of recent costume charity balls she'd attended with Peter. He'd dressed once as the Space Man in a James Bond movie, and had to travel to the outskirts of London to rent the costume. He was the hit of the party, so tall and handsome, she said. He loved wearing black-tie and showing off, and Elaine's friends were impressed. At the end of the party, about three in the morning, Elaine and her girlfriend called taxis, as they usually did, to return to their separate flats on opposite sides of London. Then they'd phone each other to report they were home. But that evening, Peter insisted, "We came together, we'll go home together." So he joined them in one taxi, first to one end of the city and then to the other, to see them both to their doors. Always the gentleman, Elaine said.

We went to Peter's office, met with HR, and reviewed abhorrent paperwork related to his death. We met with his boss, who said he and Peter had just completed a performance review, and Peter had gotten top scores and a nice raise, though Peter hadn't yet been informed. His boss called Peter a genius, capable of earning a million dollars a year before long. I wondered if Peter would have felt that in his bones.

His boss said there was one thing Peter could have worked harder on. He was quiet in group settings despite usually knowing the answers. Peter's boss had encouraged him to speak up more. I wondered if Peter would have resolved to try harder.

We went to his work space, met the colleagues who had worked near him, saw the telephone from which he had phoned us, the keyboard from which he had emailed us. Mark sank down in his chair, pulled out each drawer, and gingerly thumbed through the files of his projects, his expenses, his investments. He gathered up assorted pens (one from Minnesota), random business cards, and paper scraps with scribbled phone numbers of restaurants. This meager collection of business tools, of a career not yet fulfilled, fit into one box that Deutsche Bank would send back to Minnesota.

And we went one final time to his flat on Pembridge Crescent. In May, when we visited, the flat was vibrant with energy and the floor cluttered with opened maps as Peter prepared for the adventure ride on the Isle of Wight, but now it seemed to yawn with the absence of his physical being. Mac, bereft without his companion, planned to move. While we were at the flat, Mac asked Mark to join him on the AIDS ride in California the next spring, a ride he said he and Peter were planning to do. Now Mark and Mac would do it together in Peter's memory.

The flat was now neat, the maps of adventure stacked on the coffee table, his bed made. All that was left of London Peter was a pile of dirty laundry on the floor of his closet and, in the foyer, the picture I'd given Mac of him and Peter at the end of the X-Adventure Ride. Leaving the stuff behind for Deutsche Bank to pack up and ship, we closed the door on Peter's London flat, his home away from home.

We wept long and hard on the return flight home. Tissues wedged between us, my head on Mark's shoulder, the flight attendant mercifully left us alone in our business class seats provided by the bank. Grateful that we had been there in May, missing him so much this time, we doubted we'd ever want to visit London again. The realization of what a treasure we'd lost sank in even further.

Back home, I felt watched. Surely people were checking out the hulk of our house as they drove by, looking for signs, wondering: How's she doing? Is she out of bed? Our shell of a home must have looked so sad. I was back at work and trying to be busy, but I was half-present, unfocused, not really interested. At home, I hid. I counted on good friends, but when other acquaintances called I sometimes wouldn't return the calls. When I did go out, I was afraid I'd run into "the fringe"—people I didn't know well and with whom I didn't want to be mush. I felt eyes of judgment more than loving concern: Has she fallen apart yet?

A friend told me, "Everyone is watching you, Mary. You're showing us how to do this." Her comment made me both angry and afraid. I didn't want to be put on a pedestal. I didn't want to be an example. I just wanted to figure things out—my way.

I felt helpless and desperately alone.

Six weeks after Peter's death, my daughters and I followed through on a plan long in the making to canoe with a group of women in Minnesota's Boundary Waters. We'd had the permits for months, and the respite would be good for us, we decided. So Ann and Lyn and I—along with Mark's sister, Ruth, my college friend Susan from Santa Fe, my French friend, Francoise, and Lyn's college roommate—three twenty-somethings and four over-fifties—paddled off from the outfitter near Ely, wearing matching pink bandanas and wo-manning three Kevlar canoes.

From the moment we launched into the pristine waters along the Minnesota-Ontario border, the four-day canoe trip for me was both relaxing and challenging. Relaxing, because my daughters were in charge, and I was allowed to sit in my grief and to soak up the presence of Peter in the shimmer of the water, in the light breeze against my face, in the call of the ever-present loons. My girls did everything: plan the menu, organize the work detail, show us how to make pad thai over two camp stoves, bake a chocolate cake in a reflector oven, cook lentils for dahl while rolling dough for nan with water bottles on the hull of a canoe. They treated us like we were the teenaged girls they had counseled on many wilderness trips.

Ann was the quiet leader, talking in Lyn's ear behind the scenes, telling her who should paddle with whom the following day, while Lyn didn't hesitate to be the taskmaster. She got us up at dawn, she alone wore a watch, and she made us roll up our air mattresses before we got out to pee. She made us wait until the first rest stop for hot coffee, irking particularly Francoise, who called her the camp Nazi. The girls were managing us in the Widji Way, a camp style Peter used to call cult-like, and I for one didn't mind being treated like a twelve year old.

Despite its peaceful setting, the trip was challenging, too, and soon became a testing ground for my friendship with my college friend. The cohesion of the group grew contentious, and Susan started preaching at me. Too often in the same canoe together, she rambled on about authors and books she'd read and about theologies and theories she'd most recently espoused. Buddhism had the answer, then Neitzche, then Sue Monk Kidd. "I believe in the inherent goodness of all people . . . that goodness triumphs over evil . . . that we are all superbly resilient to withstand hardship." She had the answers for both of us, but in her certitude she belittled my grief. She wanted me to grasp lofty ideals about the whole of mankind when I was caught up in particulars of one specific crime. Still shocked by the unique ugliness of Peter's death, I was grappling with the evil of five men who had murdered my son.

At dusk at the lakeshore while we were purifying water, Susan said, "The newspapers say that Peter was killed because he was fondling

Ann, Mary, and Carolyn canoeing in the Boundary Waters.

the dancers." I was shocked, hurt, and shot back at her, "How can you be so certain? Can you believe everything the papers say? Who would have said that? Pete Steinberg didn't say that, and he was there!" I didn't know if I was more outraged because she, a smart person, was willing to believe all she read in the newspapers or because she threw the unsubstantiated report in my face, as though Peter's alleged activities explained his death.

Then and there our double-decade friendship began to falter. Susan wanted to fix me. She could not tolerate my grief or my anger, and though I desperately needed her to walk through this valley with me, to simply hold my hand and listen to me wail, I could not show her how to help me. She went home to New Mexico on a sour note.

None of that is surprising to me now. Things change. People change. We need different things from our friends at different stages in our lives. Some friends just can't fill all shoes.

Still those days in the woods soothed my open wound. I was calmed by the beauty of the earth, awed by the many shades of green in the trees, the browns of the rocks, the glints and hues of blue in the water, and comforted by the misty sunrises, the beavers splashing in front of our paddles, the glorious sunsets, the starry nights. I felt close to God. I felt swathed in his kingdom.

My daughters amazed me. My pride for them ballooned as I experienced firsthand how much they had learned away from home, how capable they were in the wilderness, and how skilled they were at managing people. They had grown up. They could take care of me.

GRIEF HAD ALREADY BECOME FOR ME a journey in getting to know myself and my world. I was mulling over my place in the world and constantly questioning who—since obviously no longer I—was in control.

I had never really questioned my faith in God. I thought religion would protect me, keep me from evil. That's why I went to church.

I hadn't grown up in a church, yet for as long as I remember I desperately longed to belong to one. As a ten-year-old I'd spend Sunday mornings in my room, reading a little red New Testament someone had given me, tossing coins up to heaven, and pleading to be noticed. In the fifth and sixth grades, I felt odd among just a handful of kids left in the classroom when most everyone else was dismissed for religious education. In junior high the girl across the street invited me to her church. Soon after, I joined the choir and contemplated becoming confirmed. My mother's response had been, "Why would you want to do that?" so I dropped the subject and stopped attending. But I continued to feel left out through high school as my friends' social lives seemed to revolve around youth activities at their churches.

My father had been Catholic but stopped going to Mass after his mother and young son died within a year of each other. For years afterward, the colorful offering envelopes came in the mail and we used them when we played library in my father's den. Before my father died, I questioned him about his agnosticism and told him I missed having a religious tradition. He admitted he might have been wrong not to have taken me to church, but on his own deathbed he felt no connection to God.

It's not surprising I attended a church-affiliated college and married a preacher's son. But Mark felt he'd had enough church in his youth, I soon learned. Though his father married us and we attended church whenever his parents visited, it wasn't until we had our own children that we felt compelled to find a church. I led the search.

We discovered the House of Hope on St. Paul's Summit Avenue on Christmas Eve, arriving just as the choir, candles in hand, was filing into the darkened sanctuary to the sweet sounds of "Silent Night." Standing in the back, me very pregnant with Peter and Mark chasing after Ann as she climbed up and down the balcony steps before falling asleep on his shoulder, we were mesmerized by the cavernous neo-Gothic sanctuary, the glorious stained-glass windows, the angelic voices, and the thundering organ. We watched as a holy theater unfolded on the chancel: scenes from the Nativity intermittently brightened and softened behind silk screens, with church members dressed in burlap or silk holding poses familiar to us from Old Master paintings—*The Anunciation* by Fra Angelico, Rembrandt's *The Angel Appearing to the Shepherds.*

Peter was so proud to be asked, once he was tall enough, maybe in the eighth grade, to be a shepherd boy in that Christmas Eve tableaux service. He served in that role for a couple years. Then finally, when he was the tallest and most willing of the teenaged boys, he got to be Gabriel, the key role, and was draped in flowing pink satin, angel wings on his back, holding high a golden trumpet, holding stock still for what felt like hours to us. He was thrilled.

We belonged. Ann, Peter, and Carolyn all sang in the children's choir, attended Sunday School, and were confirmed into membership.

Mark and I each served as officers of the church. We used to sit most weeks in the same pew near the front of the sanctuary. We watched with pride as our kids processed in robes down the aisle. I felt sheltered. I felt safe.

When Peter died, I realized I had been more interested in the intellectual and social matters of the church than I was in the spiritual matters of my soul. My prayers were shallow and self-serving. I had taken faith for granted. God, I believed, would simply be there if I ever needed him.

I wonder now if Peter's church attendance and confirmation made any difference in the end. Was his way over the horizon eased? Was he called by name any more quickly than my father, who professed not to believe? Were Peter and my father on opposite sides of some incandescent gate? I choose to think of them together, my father and my son, standing tall in the palm of God.

Peter, in front of the South Tower of the World Trade Center, September 11, 1999.

Six

Autumn 2001

On August 31, 2001, the prosecutor of Atlantic County, Murray, presented his case to a grand jury. We were not present, but the news release was faxed to Mark's office.

> A three-count indictment charges Tamer Shahid, a bouncer at the club, with murder, aggravated assault and conspiracy to commit aggravated assault in connection with the death of Peter Westra, a 24-year-old real estate mortgage [sic] broker with the Deutsche Bank in London.
>
> Shahid, 25, . . .[is] an Egyptian national who had been in the resort city for about three weeks prior to the homicide which occurred on July 8. Shahid is being held in the Atlantic County jail under $350,000 cash bail.
>
> The results of an autopsy performed on Westra indicated he died from blunt force trauma to the head and neck. The postmortem examination also indicated that there was other evidence of trauma on the legs and torso of Westra.

In the probable-cause hearing, a municipal judge ruled there was enough evidence to sustain the charges against the bouncer Pete Steinberg had identified. Shahid would remain in prison until trial. Two additional bouncers were charged with assault and conspiracy, as were the owner of the bar and the manager, but they were all released on bail. According to Murray, convictions of the four could result in five to ten years with no parole until eighty-five percent of the sentence had been served.

We felt hopeful. They had the guys, they had the charges, and they had the laws on the book for assaults on sidewalks outside strip clubs. The evidence was there, and Steinberg was an eyewitness. The case felt like a slam dunk.

Would we go, people kept asking? Of course we would, I always said. How could we not go? I was eager for Peter's day in court. I wanted his character vindicated, and his behavior that fateful night validated as totally undeserving of the vicious assault. I wanted my son to come alive again in a court of law, buoyant and joyful and friendly to everyone.

Mark, on the other hand, didn't want to attend the trial. He said it would be brutal. He didn't want glimpses of an awful death to infringe on cherished memories of a living son. Together we communicated with the prosecutor as he prepared his case for trial, and I knew there was no way my husband would not be present.

We tried to settle into the familiar rhythms of our lives, yet everything felt new and out of kilter. We continued to try . . . for Peter's sake.

In September I reached far beyond my comfort zone—Peter would have wanted me to—and decided to try the Chequamagon Fat Tire Race in northern Wisconsin, an annual competition Mark and our friends had ridden a couple of times. I'd done very little mountain biking, even though Mark had given me a new bike for my birthday in June, just a few days before Peter's death, which had since remained in the garage, unridden, unwanted.

On Labor Day we took the bikes to a local park in a feeble attempt to practice for the race. I bumped along the trail, trying to get used to the shift mechanisms and brakes so different from my road bike. I careened in the rutted tracks, leaned forward to attack the hills, and gripped the brakes to ease my way down them. The sudden downshifts and hard peddling, trying to stay on the course, reminded me of my grief journey: an unknown course with no direction other than forward and upward or downward. I was surprised by how good the biking felt on my body. A week later I actually finished the race, slower than the middle of the pack, but proud of making the effort.

I wore Peter's shirt—the two-tone green bike shirt he wore for the race on the Isle of Wight. I felt his hand on the middle of my back, pushing me up the hill and patting me in congrats at the end. I thought how proud he would be of me. I remembered how quick he was to encourage others and to congratulate achievement. I remembered how when he was twelve he jumped in and ran a few miles with me during my first Twin Cities marathon, continually talking to help me get to the finish. "Looking good, Mom . . . How you feeling, Mom?" I could hardly breathe. I was dying. All I wanted to say was, "Shut up, Peter, and keep running!"

He was there for me, always encouraging me to try new things.

ONE SUNNY MORNING IN SEPTEMBER, when I was home from work awaiting a delivery, Shelley stopped over on her bike. We sat on the patio, drank tea and talked about our child-rearing principles. I told her abstract principles didn't seem very important to me anymore. I told her how Mark and I used to agree we shouldn't provide too much financial support to our kids for fear of enabling or spoiling them, but now, with Peter's death, we might feel more generous if our help was needed. Then the phone rang.

"What are you doing?" Mark asked. "Turn on the television."

Terrorists had hit the World Trade Center. Shelley and I sat stunned in disbelief for most of the morning, glued to the television, watching the smoke and the second plane and the dust, afraid for her daughter, Bente, who was working in Washington DC, afraid for Peter's friends in New York City. While Shelley and I were questioning our child-rearing principles, terrorists were attacking the U.S. in the name of their own tightly held principles.

Peter might have been there. He had lived his first year after college just a few blocks from the World Trade Center, and the Deutsche Bank building where he worked stood on Liberty Street across from the South Tower.

We feared more bad news. Were Peter's friends and colleagues all right? Eventually we learned that no one Peter knew or we knew had perished in the attacks. I couldn't help but think, however, how outraged Peter would have been. I suspected the attacks might have strengthened his inclination to remain in Europe, or to go on to grad school; in July he seemed to have already lost his enchantment with the frenetic pace of life and work in Manhattan.

The terrorist attacks hit me hard. As the newscasts wore on, I had to admit I felt jealous. I fought a sickening sense that the tragedy of Peter's death would be overshadowed, forgotten, minimized by the great national tragedy. I wanted to see Peter's name and picture among the victims of 9-11, for Peter too was a victim of willful violence, caught in the wrong place at the wrong time. My grief for Peter was just as valid as the grief of the thousands of mothers, fathers, siblings, and friends who had lost someone in New York or Washington or on a field in Pennsylvania. I wanted everyone who loved us and loved Peter to remember him among those victims.

On the morning of October 8, three months to the day after Peter's death, Mark and I got up at four, threw on coats, and without words headed down to the dock to mark the fifty-some minutes Peter had lived after the bouncers' assault. Going to the dock had become our ritual, one we would uphold for a long time, our way of visiting Peter's grave, even when the mornings grew cold and windy with winter. We sat quietly on the wooden bench and gazed at the starlit sky. The full moon was surrounded by a huge halo, and in the halo I felt the presence of Peter. We stayed until 5:07, the time of his death. We remembered. We would never forget.

IN THE WAKE OF 9-11, LYN WANTED to come home for her fall break. She said she needed to spend time with us. We passed much of the long weekend in tears. When I asked her how she was doing after losing her brother, she said she didn't think about him much. She couldn't, she said. She had too much to do—classes, studying, a job, rugby.

"I'm not like you, Mom," she told me. "I can't let things upset me."

I let it go. I didn't want to provoke her. She was home with us because she wanted to be. No matter what she said, I didn't see how she could help but be rocked by her brother's death and the terrorist attacks. How could she put her grief, or was it fear, in a box and stuff it away? I wished Maine was not so far away.

Mark and I had both lost siblings. My sister had taken her own life when I was twenty-four; Mark's brother died suddenly of a dissection of his aorta when Mark was thirty-five. We grieved the loss of our siblings, but we were both adults, out on our own when they died. I suspected Peter's death would hit Ann and Lyn harder than the deaths of our siblings had hit us. Though we had raised our children to be independent and autonomous, I always hoped my children would be friends with each other through adulthood, closer than I had been to my own sisters. We wanted them free to try their own wings, yet we wanted to remain con-

Peter (right front) and his Middlebury College intramural soccer team making a pitch for
T-shirts from the Schlitz Brewing Company.

nected. Now, especially, I wanted us to be patient with each other. I did
not want to lose my girls.

IN OCTOBER, WE VENTURED TO VERMONT for homecoming weekend at
Middlebury. Peter's friends had planned a hike in his memory to the sum-
mit of Snake Mountain, twenty minutes from the campus, and they had
asked us to join them. We eagerly accepted, for it was another tribute to
Peter, an occasion to make him come alive again, and an opportunity to
put names to the faces of those who had come to Minnesota in July. Be-
sides, we wanted to know his friends better, and we wanted them to help
us know our son better, too.

I met Deana for coffee on the afternoon before the hike. She was
a friend who'd come to visit Peter in Minnesota during a college holiday

break. She missed the memorial service in July because she'd been study-ing in Costa Rica. When she returned to the U.S. a couple weeks later, she called and told us Peter had left a message on her cell phone en route to Atlantic City, asking when they could get together, a message she had not received until after his death. It was so typical, she said, of his efforts to stay connected.

Deana brought several photos of Peter, and I brought a few of my own. Together, often weeping, we noted how many of the pictures showed Peter standing among his friends with his long arms stretched around the shoulders of one or more friends. Then we looked at the T-shirt she'd designed for the hike. Peter—symbolized by a polar bear, his personal mascot because he lived in White Bear Lake—stood at the center, lined up with his friends, arms extending around their shoulders, each of them looking westward over Lake Champlain to the misty Adirondacks in the distance.

The next day we climbed Snake Mountain. Mark and I trudged up the hill, meandered along the pathways, and rustled through the sodden yellowed leaves while we talked privately with various friends. At the sum-mit, more than a hundred of Peter's college friends stood with us in a cir-cle, shoulder to shoulder, in solemn reflection and tribute. Jeff stepped forward. "Attending Peter's funeral was one of the most difficult events of my life. I felt like I never got to really say good-bye to him. However, when we went back to the Westras' home after the funeral, I realized he wasn't really gone. . . . And today you can feel his presence again. Peter is still with us all."

I WAS SOBERED AND SADDENED for these happy-go-lucky kids. They were so irrevocably changed, suddenly grown up, their innocence lost, not only by the untimely violent death of their friend, but also by the tragedy of 9-11.

I felt the reality and finality of Peter's death during that weekend at Middlebury. His friends were kind to include us—they would for years—but homecoming at Middlebury was not about us. The hike was in memory of Peter, but he was not the glue that bound them, and, as his parents, we were almost intruders. The weekend was about them—friends being together, renewing bonds, moving on. For them, I thought, life goes on.

Peter's friends had set an example, but I was not yet ready to be carried along. Back home, we muddled in the morass of grief. Day after day I dragged myself out of bed, mechanically grabbed one drab outfit or another, slipped around my neck the white-bear-on-gold-chain that reminded me of Peter, and headed off to work. I was relieved to have someplace to go, for I couldn't stand my own company. But though I hated being alone, I dreaded being with people. Mark said it perfectly: "I just can't stop thinking about Peter."

I felt the pressure "to be healed" and "to get over" my loss. I felt pushed . . . by my colleagues, by my friends, even by our good friend Steve, who had been at our home within the first hour.

"Mary, you've just got to find a way to get through this."

"How?" I howled.

"I don't know."

I sensed whispers in the crowds around me saying, "Life is for the living." But that chorus rang hollow for me. I felt abandoned by life, half-dead, full of self-pity. Poor me. I didn't want to get back to normal! And anyway, what was normal? What would I get back to? I didn't want to forget the pain, the loneliness, the loss of Peter. I was terrified Peter would be forgotten.

Some days I pushed myself, made a supreme effort. Then I'd dig in my heels and shut down. I'd want to scream, "My son is dead!"

One day on public radio I heard lines from Rumi, the thirteenth century Islamic mystic. "Grief is a cleansing, a shredding, a healing that makes us more alive . . . a scouring down to the bare soul." Would I find my soul, I wondered? Or would I wash down the drain with the cleansing and the scouring?

I felt so different from everyone around me, intact people, people who had it together. I felt like I was on a pedestal—superior in my grief, entitled to be honest and open, capable of showing others how to deal with misfortune—but also in a pit of despair that no one else could possibly understand. I didn't think anyone really cared.

What was I supposed to learn from this suffering?

I craved validation for what I used to be—a good person and a good mom, I hoped—and for what I was still trying to become—a good mom and a good person. Yet I suspected no one needed my lessons packed as they were with self-righteous overtones. No one wanted to hear from a woman who'd been burned, who'd failed. It felt like quite the fall for the high school senior who'd been voted Most Dignified by her peers.

I wanted patience, good ears, hand holding, and love . . . just like everyone else.

I OBSESSED ABOUT HOW IMPATIENT I had been with Peter when he was growing up. How often did I opt out of my parenting role because it felt difficult or because I was scared? I remember finding the *Playboys* under his mattress when he was twelve, and then calling Mark to make him be the one to talk to our son.

He did not allow us to help him during his college application process, which hurt me. He did not share his essays, which we knew were difficult for him to write; he went to his friends and his college counselor for help.

I had made so many mistakes. I wish I had applauded his violin playing. He was never shy about playing but wasn't terribly good, and I had wanted him to take it more seriously. Now I realized he was good enough.

And why hadn't I taken Nordic skiing more seriously when I had the chance to learn from him? I had tried to follow in his tracks, to model myself after his rhythmic strides, but I got so tired, and he got so far ahead of me. I gave up. Now, after his death, I was taking lessons from strangers and forcing myself to get out alone to practice.

I wished I could smell his dirty socks again! I'd gladly do all his laundry without complaint.

One day during his college years, he stood next to me in the kitchen. I was hurrying to chop onions as he took his time cutting every bit of fat off the chicken we were about to cook together. When I told him he was too fussy about the fat, he turned to me, put his hands on my shoulders, and told me, "Take it easy, Mom."

Why was everything so trivial then and so utterly serious now? Couldn't I have another chance, Peter?

Seven

Holidays

We had become members of the Club—parents who had lost children. This was no formal organization, just an impromptu network of mostly mothers, many of whom called me and offered sympathy. Though I abhorred the concept, I could not have done without the empathy—coffee, good ears, and strong shoulders—from other mothers who had lost children. Their words soothed me more than any drug and offered me advice I needed.

"Just remember, Mary, you can't be Peter," Josie said as we sat holding hands in the coffee shop at the museum. She had lost her accomplished government-employee daughter in an airplane crash more than a decade earlier, yet tears streamed down her face as she told me how her daughter continued to inspire her daily. "You'll never be able to bike like him, or run a marathon for him, or take his place in your husband's heart," she warned me.

Meech told me how she had pleaded with her dead son on her way to work. "Not now, Seany. I just can't think about you right now." Subsequent breast cancer was *nothing*, she emphasized, compared to the sudden death of her teenaged son in an auto accident. Bobbi told me she lost her short-term memory for months and did not feel real joy again until she held her first grandchild. Lois confided she hadn't worn lipstick for a full year after the death of her daughter. Ingrid invited me over to see the memorial garden she'd planted in memory of her son, adorned with a ribbon around a tree and a street sign proclaiming "Martin's Lane."

Peter as Gabriel in a Christmas Eve tableaux service.

One mother told me she was writing about her only son, who had been killed in a mountain-climbing accident. When I asked if she'd share her work with me, she replied, "You don't want to read my story. You've got your own story to live."

They all seemed so brave to me, these mothers-friends-kindred spirits. I felt honest, uninhibited, and genuine in their presence, free to wail. I hung on their every word and gained insight into my own feelings. All of them inspired me and were models for me. Now when I reach out to others more newly bereaved than I, I remember their examples.

I went back to the therapist we had seen a few years before for help with our marriage. Mark went with me a couple times but then stopped because he said he didn't have anything to talk to her about. The therapist helped me understand our different styles of grieving—my compulsion to talk about feelings and Mark's need to lock his feelings up and throw away the key.

I also went a few times to the community grief group sponsored by my church. I didn't think I was repressing any feelings, but I trusted my automatic pilot to take me to the meeting if I needed to be there. I felt dismayed when I saw people who were five, six, even ten years away from the loss of their child, still pining. I was frightened it would take me as long to "get over" my loss. Once there, I wanted most to be home with Mark.

Every parent warned the holidays would be awful. So after some discussion, the four of us decided we didn't want to be four in our big house, which had always cradled five of us, afraid we'd be too sad. The girls expressed fear we would be pulled in too many different directions, meaning, I thought, too many people would stop by if we were home. I think the girls were worried they wouldn't get enough of Mark and me for themselves.

So over that first Thanksgiving we hunkered down together for four days at a home in Hilton Head offered by friends. It became a refuge for relaxation and reflection, in which we reorganized, walked and biked the beach, Rollerbladed, and played golf. We were gentle with each other, supersensitive of each other's raw emotions barely held in check. So much went unsaid. No one talked about missing Peter or about the photos I'd brought along in a desperate effort to keep him a part of the family. Our grief, I suspect, was still too new for words.

I dreaded Christmas. Both girls would be home for only the second time since their brother's death. They made it clear they wanted as normal a Christmas as possible, yet I struggled to understand what the new normal in our changed family would be.

The girls wanted a tree, which they'd help us decorate when they got home. They wanted Christmas cookies. They wanted simple gifts. I got it—they wanted the family traditions to continue. They didn't want Peter's death to destroy everything. I'd try . . . but it would be a fainthearted effort.

December used to be such a frenetic month in our household when the kids were young. We'd shop early, as a family, for the plumpest tree on the lot. Some years we'd muscle a majestic sixteen-footer into our front foyer. Mark would have to haul in the big ladder from behind the garage to put on the lights, and the rest of us would hang over the second-floor railing to arrange, and sometimes to fling, the ornaments on the tree. I used to wrap gifts in color-coordinated paper—green for Ann, red for Peter, white for Lyn—and I kept on hand years' worth of heavy-duty blue-with-white-stars paper for gifts from Santa. We decorated gingerbread houses and cutout sugar cookies, each of us in a Christmas apron. When she was still in high school, Lyn eagerly waited for her siblings to arrive home from college. One year she strung lights around Peter's room to welcome her brother home.

This year, well into December, the refrigerator was empty and the tree stood in the corner of the family room, strung with lights but devoid of decorations. In one of the boxes from London, I'd seen a basket containing ornaments I'd sent to Peter over the years, snowmen and santas on skis, several polar bears, evidence from the tiny packages of ornaments I used to mail between Thanksgiving and Christmas to our kids at college. I dug out the basket and hung each of Peter's ornaments tenderly, one by one, on a patch at the center front of the tree where Mark and I could admire them from the couch, and left the remainder of our family ornaments until the girls got home. I hung Peter's stocking with the others on the fireplace mantel in the living room. How could I not? Peter would always be a member of this family.

At four in the morning on the eighth of December, Mark and I went down to the dock, a stack of wooden planks on the shoreline in wintertime. The morning felt forlorn, gray. There was no ice in sight, rather late for the season in Minnesota, and I couldn't help but think that maybe Peter was keeping the water warm.

I didn't send holiday cards, and I wasn't sure I ever would again. I forced myself to hang the six frames full of holiday photos recording more than twenty-three years of our best family times. There . . . in the first frame . . . Ann in red-and-white polka dot pajamas that Grandma had made. The next year . . . Peter wearing the same pajamas.

The dining-room table remained jumbled with photos, notes, and memorabilia of Peter that had accumulated since the memorial service. I knew the girls would expect to eat dinner in the dining room, but I felt paralyzed as to how to clear it. I intended to get the clutter organized, to make photo albums and scrapbooks, but I couldn't summon the energy.

Then my friend Kris suggested I make photo albums for the girls— just the spark I needed. I spent many evenings after work choosing, copying, and pasting photos of each girl with her brother and a few family shots into two leather albums. In the cutout cover of each album I placed a photo of Peter with his sister. It was fun to do. I felt like I was repaying my daughters for their assemblage of photos in the week after Peter's death.

I sorted the remainder of papers and photos from the table into three shallow boxes—Peter through high school, Peter in college, and Peter after college—and piled the boxes on my desk. Then I spread the evergreen-colored tablecloth over the dining table.

The Saturday before Christmas was dreary, cloudy, like snow wanted to fall but couldn't, and I kept thinking Peter would arrive on the afternoon flight from London. Mark and I were anxious for the girls to get home, knocking around at loose ends while we waited. Then about a dozen of Peter's high school friends showed up with pizza. We pulled a few beers out of the fridge, tossed a salad, and sat around the kitchen table, talking about Peter, about high school, about how the friends were growing up, about how Peter nearly grew up too. We talked about upcoming marriages. We guffawed and we groaned, adoring every moment of each other's company.

Mark was wearing one of Peter's favorite sweaters, one with a complicated Norwegian pattern. Ellen, one of the group of friends, had knit it, so we asked her how the sweater came to be. She told us of going with Peter to select the yarn while they were on break their freshman year of college. She had to talk him out of bright blue and yellow and into regal blue, gray, and burgundy which looked great on Peter and now looked good on Mark. A few weeks later, Ellen would bring over hats of the same pattern and colors for Mark, Ann, Carolyn, and me.

The high school friends made us feel like Peter's parents again. We told them we had established a fund at their school in Peter's memory, but were stuck on defining its purpose. "Peter loved sports. It should be something to do with sports," one said.

"He loved so many sports. It would be hard to choose one," said another.

"But the gear . . . remember how he loved the gear? How many pairs of skis did he have anyway?"

"Remember when he showed up for a ski meet in tweedy old knickers and a long grungy turtleneck sweater? Where did he get those?" I told the group how I had made the knickers from a pair of my father's old wool pants.

"And all those fancy sunglasses and athletic bags . . ."

That evening we decided together the purpose of the fund should be to help kids afford the equipment they needed for athletic activities. Even at the private school the kids had attended, some families needed help with new skates or skis or warm-up jerseys, de rigueur for varsity sports. And we would focus on Nordic skiing since that was Peter's major endeavor.

At the door, we doled out hugs as well as T-shirts from the Middlebury hike, the ones that showed a polar bear and Peter's name. I told the kids, "To the Middlebury gang we're still Mr. and Mrs. Westra, but to you guys, high school friends, we'll always be Mary and Mark." Mark said, "Come back, anytime."

When Ann and Carolyn arrived home the next day, we drove to Duluth to visit Mark's mom, who was on her deathbed in a nursing home. We were in a motel on Christmas Eve morning when I woke up suddenly. In the dark I was confused, not remembering where I was, but still aware of the subtle presence of Peter. I sensed a shadow of his body, mostly his back, so close I could touch him. He turned around and told me he would be crying too. He would miss celebrating Christmas with us. I reached out to touch the tears on his cheeks . . . and then I woke up, weeping.

On our way out of Duluth, we stopped to see Grandma again. She looked frail, so tired her head drooped. I kissed her and whispered "good morning" and "rest well," but it felt like "good-bye." I was tempted to tell her to say hello to Peter. She would get to be with him soon, and I wished I had been able to say "good-bye" and "rest well" to my son. I wished I too could see him again soon.

On Christmas Eve at church we sat in the back pew for the tableaux service in which Peter used to take part. The lights were dimmed, dulling the glitter of the holiday garb, and the candles glowed as the sanctuary grew dark. The four of us held hands and wiped tears from our faces as theater of the Nativity unfolded from the front. I saw Peter as

Gabriel behind a silk screen on the chancel stage, billowing pink satin, shimmering golden wings, trumpet held high. He was now one of the angels for whom we sang.

Oh, we missed him that Christmas. In the morning Mark and I were in tears before we got out of bed to get our stockings, before the girls came to plop themselves on our bed with their stockings. We all noticed the extra room on the bed that Peter used to fill with his long legs.

For dinner we made sweet potatoes the way he used to make them—cutting up the cooked potatoes, layering the slices in a casserole, dotting them with butter and pecans and marshmallows—wondering if he was watching over his dad's shoulder at the broiler to make sure the marshmallows didn't burn. At the dining table we passed a candle around so each of us could in turn light a candle in the pewter heart-shaped holders by our plates, saying his name aloud and expressing a word of gratitude. It was awkward, but the remembrance felt like an accomplishment, doing something, just a little something, to keep Peter in our midst.

Rather than resolutions, for New Year's Eve our family made predictions. Ann would do such-and-such by the end of the year; a certain politician would win the election; a favored athletic team would win a major contest. We recorded the predictions on paper we tucked away with the Christmas wrapping, revisiting the predictions the following year to see who was correct. This year we didn't dare predict the future of anything.

We wished we could forget 2001. But we knew 2002 would not be any better. It would be the year of the trial. After the holidays we would begin to hear more about it from New Jersey. That night, I resolved simply to try to live each day, each moment, as honestly and as fully as I could.

Lyn turned twenty-one on January 4. We had her favorite dinner, her choice of cake, and a few presents, before she prepared to go out for the evening with her friends.

As she was leaving, I panicked.

"Be careful, Lyn."

"Mom, I'll be fine."

I was asleep when she knocked on our bedroom door at almost three in the morning.

"Mom, I'm home."

She'd been in "some random bar" but everything was "all right," she said. I could smell the beer on her breath, but I hugged her tightly. I was not going to complain about Lyn waking me to report that she was home . . . and safe.

When she got her wisdom teeth pulled a few days later, I stayed home from work to take care of her. Normally feisty and independent, she didn't complain one whit about my bringing her milkshakes and apple-sauce, changing her cold packs, serving her painkillers. Maybe my role as mother in this family was not totally, irretrievably diminished, I hoped.

Hope is so elusive to the bereaved. In the dark days of early January, Mark and I talked about hope. "It isn't that I don't feel hopeful," he said. "It's just that I can't stop thinking about Peter." I hated to see my spouse suffer, but I felt helpless. This was going to take awhile, I thought. Six months was nothing. If Peter were still an infant, at six months he'd be crawling. And so were we . . . crawling.

So where was the hope? I didn't know . . . but it wasn't in Christmas or the New Year. Hope was being a good mom for my daughters, who didn't need me in the way they used to but who still deserved my love and support. I vowed to capitalize on the mothering moments, give hugs and kisses whenever I could, offer "shoulds" and "coulds" but not be offended if my advice was ignored. I hoped to have the good sense to remain quiet so they could discover their own paths, and I hoped to simply be there to applaud them or to catch them. I hoped to be more than a mother to my daughters: a friend, a peer, or a partner when appropriate. And, above all, I hoped to be a staunch supporter and partner to my best friend, Mark.

IN MID-JANUARY, MARK AND I went to New York City for several days to attend the antiques sales and auctions that constitute American Antiques Week. Being there felt a bit like it had the year before when we spent time with Peter. I found myself looking for him everywhere. All the tall young men, all the black coats, all the briefcases and cell phones—all reminded me of Peter. I did double takes, searching.

I had asked Peter's friend Molly to join me at the Fifth Avenue Spa in celebration of the Christmas gift Peter had given me the year before, such a classy gift, I thought, for a son to give his mother. I would memorialize that gift for several years by taking one of his friends to the spa until Ann moved to New York and was able to join me. That Friday afternoon, Molly and I held hands during our pedicures and we talked about Peter. She told me about their plans to share an apartment before he got transferred to London, about how they were passed over by several landlords who didn't consider them serious prospects for long-term rental. So, they decided to hold hands while looking at apartments in order to appear to be a couple, which they weren't, to get a more positive response. But then Peter moved to London. While we sat in terrycloth robes, waiting for our nails to dry, Molly, married now to one of Peter's friends present in Atlantic City, confided hopes, regrets, and dreams.

New York was no longer the same city since September 11. It was a sad place, with photos and stories posted everywhere in tribute to victims of the terrorist attacks. Mark and I stopped in the downtown church just blocks from Peter's John Street apartment, one he must have walked past daily en route to the Deutsche Bank building, and noted the pictures and memorabilia and lists of lost loved ones, arranged alphabetically by victim. Mark slowed as he passed the W's. He found "Peter West" . . . so close. We identified with every picture, every memorial, and I wept in acknowledgment of July 8 as my September 11. I shared the grief of thousands of parents and bereft survivors who were themselves victims of wanton, cruel, and intentional violence. "It's not just six thousand lives lost. It's one life lost six thousand times," said a rabbi in the first days after the attacks. One life, but I felt like I'd lost my son a thousand times during that visit to New York City.

One afternoon we had coffee with Peter's friend Rowan, a film school student who lived across the street from Peter's downtown apartment. She had recruited him to star in her final class project, and after his memorial service, but before 9-11, we received her video, "The Commuter"—two-and-a-half minutes of Peter on Rollerblades in Manhattan, coming out of his apartment, sitting down on the step and tying his laces, smoothing his tie, putting on his headset, and cruising off to his office building. It was a hit in her film class, she said, and Peter was a natural actor. After 9-11, the film had significance not only because of Peter's death but also for the devastation of the neighborhood it was shot in. Rowan also sent us a photo of Peter standing on the rooftop of an apartment building with the South Tower looming behind him, the only photo of the World Trade Center she had taken that Sunday morning when

Peter helped her use up her film from class. She told us the photo was taken 9-11-99. We gasped . . . too uncanny, too spooky.

We were going to meet Peter's Deutsche Bank colleagues for lunch at Citarella's at Fifty-fourth and Sixth. I was nervous. We walked up the stairs and approached the table and suddenly eight young men in blue oxford-cloth shirts stood to greet us. Tears rolled down my cheeks. Peter should to be there too. The colleagues were polite, soft spoken. They described working in the investment banking world, the long hours of the first years, the drag their careers had on their social lives. They all agreed it was just as well to be working evenings, because if they weren't working, they were spending money, lots of money, since evenings in Manhattan were expensive. I used to feel sorry for Peter, imagining him hunkered down at his desk for two or more meals a day, tucked away, alone in his cubicle. I felt better when they told us they ordered meals in and ate dinner together as colleagues in a conference room. In spite of the horrendous hours, Peter had had a social life of sorts.

We met his Middlebury friends at Raoul's in Soho, the restaurant where we'd dined with Peter the year before. It was the first of several reunions with his friends in New York City, for we'd meet them, in one configuration or another, for dinner for the next several years when we attended American Antiques Week. We felt embraced by his friends and close to Peter, but I might have set a tone with them I didn't intend. When the waitress came to take drink orders, I spoke up quickly to request bubbly water with lime. After that, no one else ordered alcohol either. I didn't mean to preach or to imply they shouldn't drink in the wake of their friend's alcohol-related death. Afterward, I could hear Peter say, "Lay off my friends, Mom."

Those Middlebury friends needed us as much as we needed them. They knew Peter better than we did in the last few years, and we still had much to learn through their tales. They too were concerned about the pending trial and wanted to support us. And we all wanted to support Pete Steinberg, Peter's friend, the eyewitness from the bachelor party who knew the most and would have to tell the most about that hour in Atlantic City.

On the last morning we were in New York, I got up before Mark and walked a couple blocks to attend the Sunday service at the Fifth Avenue Presbyterian Church, the church where Deutsche Bank and Middlebury had held a memorial service for Peter. The pastor's introit was a passage about gathering the lost sheep. He compared looking for sheep to retracing the steps of lost loved ones in New York City. He talked about mourning the missing ones. I realized I too was retracing steps of my lost one, like many visitors to the city in the months after 9-11. The service concluded with "For the Beauty of the Earth"—the same hymn we had sung in July at our church. After the service, I sat quietly for a long while in the chapel, pondering the weight of the message and the sadness of the place.

That night I dreamed of Peter. I saw him come slowly down the aisle of an auditorium, or a church, maybe that church, dressed in the olive-green cable-knit sweater he had worn when we saw him in London— a sweater I now wear at times. He was flanked on either side by throngs of other young people, also dressed casually. From where we stood in the fourth or fifth pew, next to the aisle, Mark and I turned to watch Peter approach. The aisle was sloped so that he seemed almost to descend toward us. He was shorter than I remembered him, with a sheepish grin on his face and his hair mussed. He was looking at us as he walked down the aisle, and when he approached, he stopped and gave us each a hug.

"How are you?" he asked.

"Fine," we said. "How are you?"

"Fine," he said, and then he walked on.

Eight

Birthday

D*ear Extended Family,*

Christmas is over. We made it. Now we await his birthday, the anniversary of his death, other Christmases, weddings, other funerals. We sincerely thank you for your greetings and gifts, though we did not send any to you this year.

You have asked what you can do to help us. As you know, grief does not end. You surely must miss him too. After all, you knew him when he was a babe in arms, had gangly legs and arms, funny teeth, stupid antics. You can help us by talking about Peter, with us or among yourselves, saying his name aloud, sharing thoughts and memories (and dreams, if you've been lucky enough to have them) that may creep into your daily life, at any time, month to month, this year or next. Peter is ever present in our minds. We will not forget him. You will not make us feel bad or sad if you mention him or his death. In fact, talking about him helps us enormously.

We realize Peter was no more special than your special loved ones. He was devilish and sometimes selfish, as well as generous and often fun. But he met a very tragic, untimely death, wholly undeserved, and we have months if not years of court proceedings ahead of us in which to try to seek some justice. Please feel free to ask questions.

Nothing will bring Peter back. But talking and sharing helps us remember him. And memories are all we have! We need you desperately. You are among our remaining special loved ones.

With love, Mary and Mark

Peter's sixth birthday.

Our circle of friends had often mentioned Peter's name over the holidays, several wrote about him in their cards, and Peter's friends had brought him to life for us, if only for a while. But our families treated Mark, Ann, Lyn and me as though nothing had happened. Peter was the elephant in the room, and being in their company was uncomfortable for us.

I had hoped for stronger strands of communication to open between my mother and myself, for she was a mother who had endured the loss of two children: David, her only son, was only two years old when he died of polio exactly nine months before I was born, and my oldest sister, Betty, was thirty-two, with three children, when she took an overdose of prescription drugs. My mother rarely talked about David, though his picture hung on the wall of my parents' bedroom wall with those of the other babies. We had all been confused by Betty's suicide. When it happened I was clueless, twenty-four and newly married, living half a continent away. I certainly had not understood the seriousness of her declining mental health. As I neared thirty-two years myself, at home with two small children, I dreaded I might come down too with what could have been an inherited family disease.

My mother ached for me, I'm certain, but she was not a woman of many words. She did not openly express sympathy. Even when my face was wet with tears, she would not comment unless I did first. She seemed to have long ago become inured, crusted over, incapable of speaking of loss. I wished for more empathy, some comfort on her bony shoulder, but I knew my bereavement was not going to change my ninety-year-old mother. I took comfort in her quiet presence.

IT WAS FEBRUARY AND THE TRIAL was scheduled for August. For six months we'd heard little from Atlantic City other than the gentle kind voice of Jackie, the victim witness coordinator, who phoned every month or so to see how we were doing.

Now we began to hear every couple weeks from the prosecutor's office—details from hearings, requests for evidence, plans for the prosecution. We tried not to focus on the upcoming trial, but it hung over us always, terrifying us. One night when I was exhausted but afraid I wouldn't be able to fall asleep, again, I sat late into the night in the cushy white chair next to the table in our bedroom, where I'd placed Peter's picture and a little white bear, my tiny altar of sorts. I opened my journal and let my emotions rip. As if I might control them by calling them out, I listed my fears:

- people I don't know
- questions about my family ("How many children do you have?")
- people who know me but who do not know about Peter
- people who know me who are not thinking about Peter
- heights and ski lifts (I honestly think I might jump)
- falling and accidents and killing someone with my car

- losing Mark or Carolyn or Ann but also hemming them in by those fears
- justice not being done
- my son's good reputation being dragged through the mud.

I was mostly afraid of forgetting Peter, of my friends forgetting Peter, of the girls forgetting Peter. I wanted to talk about him constantly and show my pictures. I wanted to brag. I wanted to tell everyone how vibrant he was, how many friends he made and cherished, how many lives he touched. I needed to take some credit for the good person he was in spite of the horrible way he died. I suspect I was banking all the details of Peter's good reputation in order to cushion the testimony we were sure to hear about his death.

I was afraid of learning about the blood and gore of that night, of imagining the pain Peter might have suffered, of getting images in my brain I would not be able to erase. In the fall Pete Steinberg had tried to tell us everything about that night in Atlantic City. He offered to e-mail the girls and share his notes. But it was too early. We weren't ready then for the graphic details, and I wasn't ready now. I wanted to solidify the memories of the living, loving Peter Westra before I had to endure the scene of his death in a courtroom.

Peter's birthday was approaching, and we fretted over how to mark it. I wanted to hear Peter's name and know that his life was remembered, yet the prospect of organizing something public for others made me feel selfish. Did I need to force others to remember?

My answer came during a memorial concert for the daughter of friends. I envied the mom as she held up a picture of her daughter and talked about her musical accomplishments. My mind wandered while I listened to performances by young pianists and violinists, and I wondered if an event like this would suit Peter. Before long I heard his voice telling me quite bluntly, "Give it up, Mom. Don't do it. Don't force others to think about me. I will make my friends think about me when I'm ready. You don't need to interfere."

I resolved to trust Peter. His friendships were sincere and he had touched lives in ways I couldn't completely understand. I didn't need to toot his horn. Peter was private, discreet, and disliked fanfare or fuss. He would stay in touch with those who mattered to him in his own ways.

Mark's mother died two days before our first of Peter's birthdays without him—the toughest one, what would have been his twenty-fifth. That we would have to deal with her funeral on top of our dead son's birthday struck me as unfair, but I should know better than anyone that we don't get to choose these dates. Be accepting, be gracious, trust, I told myself. At least we'd been able to say our good-byes to Mark's mom, said them many times.

Because the girls had come home for their grandmother's funeral, they were with us for Peter's birthday. I kept confusing the days, bracing, preparing for a funeral, but thinking of Peter. Flowers arrived at our house for Peter's birthday . . . or were they for Mark's mom? I was supposed to be talking about Edna Westra, but I could think only of Peter.

I told myself to think instead about Mark, to bear with him, hold his hand, support his heart. He was planning a funeral and preparing a eulogy, but he too was thinking about Peter, his son who would have turned twenty-five on Sunday, February 3. Mark had lost brother, father, son, and now mother.

We were in church on Peter's birthday, clutching Kleenex in the back pew, admiring the enormous bouquet we'd ordered—huge yellow mums and blue delphiniums—that glowed like a beacon from the communion table. As she walked down the center aisle to the front, Darlene looked our way and nodded slightly. She included loving words of comfort in a prayer we understood to be in part for us. We left church satiated with love and support from pastors who continued to hold us in prayers, prayers for which we still felt much need.

By the end of the afternoon, we had a houseful of our friends and Peter's friends, some we invited and some who simply showed up. Family photo albums were laid out and opened on the round table in the family room, "The Commuter" was running on the television, and Ann and Lyn served chocolate zucchini cake they made because it had been Peter's favorite.

Charlie brought a gigantic brilliant bouquet of twenty-five gerbera daisies in bright orange, yellow, and red, which we put in the center of the table. When friends departed, she invited each to take a daisy and go down to the lake to drop the flower on the ice, if they felt so inclined, as a memorial to Peter since his ashes were under the ice. Charlie and Bob were the last to leave at the end of the afternoon. They too went down to the lake with daisies. Driving away, Charlie called me on her cell phone.

"Mary, have you been down to the lake yet? Oh Mary, you've got to go see."

Mark and I, Ann and Lyn, put on our jackets and took the remaining bright gerbera daisies down the hill to the lake. Sure enough, there on the snow and ice, next to the stack of wood planks from the dock, was etched a snow angel—big-skirted, wide-stretched wings surrounded by flowers and emblazoned with his name—PETER. We had been visited by angels.

It had been such a grand party, full of friends and laughter and hugs, on Super Bowl Sunday, a coincidence Peter would have appreciated. I couldn't have enjoyed it more if it had been my own birthday. Everybody talked about him, joyously, jubilantly. For the day, he was alive.

Then, that evening, reality crashed in. We had no cause for celebration! Peter did not turn twenty-five! Mark and I wept in each other's arms for much of the night.

Gloom traveled with us the next morning as the four of us drove to Sioux Falls, South Dakota, for Mark's mother's funeral. There wasn't much conversation in the car. I was so exhausted by sadness, I couldn't keep my eyes open.

Mark stood ramrod straight at the door of the Presbyterian church where his father used to preach and had been eulogized five years earlier. He stoically greeted the dozens of Dutch relatives who came to pay respects to his mother, nearly every one of them, he told me later, commenting on his son's death. Mark was composed until the very end of his eulogy.

"My mother was famous among us four kids for her pithy little lessons," he told those who had come. "Once when I was in a boyish tirade about things just not being fair, she calmly retorted, 'Well, Mark, the fair doesn't come until September.'" Then Mark choked on his final words. "As many of us have learned in the last few months, life is not always fair."

In funereal procession we drove sixty miles to Hull, Iowa, where Edna would be buried between her husband Peter and her son John. We pulled into a tidy, tiny, iron-gated Dutch Reformed cemetery with Westra antecedents laying in nearly every green curved row. During the final prayer at Edna's gravesite, standing solemnly with my family, I was suddenly compelled to turn around. I looked over my shoulder for Peter, for I had a wonderful sense of his presence. Maybe he was there. Maybe Peter was showing us his place among all the Westra family gone before: his grandfather, Peter, his great-grandfather, John, his great-grandmother, Minnie, his uncle John, and now his grandmother, Edna. Surely Peter was there.

As our Jeep crawled out of the cemetery, one of the last cars to leave, I noticed a truck waiting just behind the hedge, the shadow of a man inside, ready to move in to complete the burial. As soon as we passed, the truck pulled out. The driver's face was dark and unclear, his body big, and I had the uncomfortable sense that driver was Peter. Was Peter waiting to spread the soil over his grandmother's grave?

A COUPLE MORNINGS LATER, ON FEBRUARY 8—seven months after Peter's death—I woke, wide-eyed, at four. I tried to lie still for a while to not wake Mark, but then I slipped out of bed and out of the bedroom, put a coat and boots on over my pjs, and headed down to the lake. The air was warm for February, quiet and calm, so lifeless compared to summer. I searched the horizon for signs of Peter's presence. My neck craned toward the stars, my head full of favorite lines from Saint Exupery—*in one of the stars I shall be living and in one of the stars I shall be laughing*—and tried to imagine Peter living and laughing in one of the stars.

But I felt so desperately alone. Why couldn't I capture his image tonight? Why couldn't I find Peter's face for just a moment?

Then, out of the black, I saw the bright tail of a shooting star stream across the heavens. A gift . . . another sign of Peter. I walked briskly back up the hill to the house, crawled into bed, and hugged my sleeping Mark.

I was ready for my day.

Nine

Spring Already

A month later, March 8, another anniversary, I woke up screaming. I felt as if I were falling through water or through air, falling too fast, gasping for breath. I got up, threw on my sweats and Mark's dirty socks, the moccasins Peter had given me for my last birthday, my coat and scarf. I went down to look for my son at the lake. The air was still. I felt not a whiff of his presence, yet somehow I felt peaceful. I talked to him for a while and I prayed. Then I returned to the house and climbed back into bed to warm myself by the heat of my husband's body.

I couldn't sleep. Mark and I were leaving early that morning anyway for the airport, for Paris, where we would meet Lyn for her spring break. Suddenly in a panicky sweat, I realized the genesis of my nightmare. What if the plane crashed? What if we died?

I got up and scratched a hasty note to the girls. Unable to bear the thought of their living without us, certain that Mark and I would die on our way to Paris, I scribbled a tearful one-page message and left it on the center of Ann's desk so that she'd find it if we didn't come back.

What would the girls do without their brother or their parents? How would they cope? Would our friends adopt them into their families? Would our daughters pursue their dreams? Would they feel the presence of their mother on each step of their journey, as I have felt my son's presence on every step of my own?

Would I want to lose them to be again with him?

Mark's heart had gone into atrial fibrillation for the second time in four months. He drove off to work one morning without telling me he felt ill, and went directly to the emergency room instead of his office. When I got to the hospital the nurses were hooking him up to defibrillator paddles. Medication alone, we had learned during his first bout in December, would not resettle his heart's rhythm. Mark looked brave, resigned. In December, I had found him laying on the gurney with tears in his eyes. "I just keep seeing Peter dying alone in the emergency room." I wasn't surprised his body was balking again. He'd been working on seven sets of tax returns: one for his mother, one for Carolyn, ours, and five for Peter—UK 2001, UK 2002, US Federal, NY State, and Peter's estate. My heart ached for him.

Mark's way was to work—ten-hour days, even on weekends if we didn't have plans. He didn't like to come home to an empty house, so he was rarely there when I wasn't. But he didn't complain about his lot, at least not outwardly, at least not to me. Whereas I wore my heart on my sleeve and wailed aloud, Mark tucked his grief in a box and buried it in his heart. After six months of grief therapy, I was beginning to understand the difference in our grieving styles. He was done with counselors, didn't want to read a thing, didn't choose to put words to his sadness. Maybe he thought he was setting a good example for me—showing me another way of coping and moving *on* from grief. At the same time, I told myself I was trying to set an example for him—feeling it, suffering, moving *through* grief.

I HAD DECIDED TO QUIT MY JOB at the museum. Starting so late in life after being a stay-at-home mom for more than a dozen years, I wasn't as committed to my career as Mark was to his and my earning power didn't come close. I had gone back to work because I felt too present in my teenagers' lives, and, frankly, I was bored with tennis and marathon training. Volunteer work and substitute teaching had left me unfulfilled, and I felt well-suited to working in fundraising for the arts. I loved talking to donors, planning recognition events, and making people feel good about their philanthropy. I welcomed the challenge of achieving multimillion-dollar goals each year, and after five years at the museum, I was respected by donors and coworkers.

But the fundraising climate had changed after 9-11, people were not as generous, and being the recipient of gifts to two funds in Peter's memory had made me realize that philanthropy had less to do with the nudge of development officers than the passion of donors.

I had a specific impetus for wanting to quit. A promotion in my department had gone to a coworker whom I didn't trust but who would now be my boss. I felt demoted and under-valued, forced to deal with another loss I didn't want. All the cockeyed, misdirected anger I'd been harboring for months about losing my son blasted out of me. How could they treat me this way? Didn't they know I couldn't work for that woman? Were they willing to lose me?

Supercilious in my grief, I took the "department restructuring" personally, even though I was told I shouldn't. When I calmed down, I went to human resources, consulted a career counselor, and talked at length with Mark, who just wanted me to be happy. "I'm happy when you're happy, Mary," he always told me. I would need the time anyway, we agreed, to get ready for the encroaching trial.

I resigned two weeks later, on our return from vacation, and departed after that with grace. I had weighed the pros and the cons, and I felt proud to be emboldened to exercise control over a job situation I hadn't foreseen and didn't want. But it's clear to me now it was still a knee-jerk reaction in anger over Peter's death, an effort to re-assert some control in the process of grief.

THAT MARCH, WE SETTLED IN PARIS with Lyn in a tiny one-and-a-half bedroom apartment in the Marais, not far from the Picasso Museum. Lyn had wanted to visit friends who were studying for a semester in London, but we were not yet ready to return to where Peter had lived, so the three of us agreed on a week together in Paris before Lyn went alone to England.

Arm-in-arm with Lyn we tromped the streets of Paris. We bought baguettes and cheese, stopped in parks, visited museums. Lyn and I got sassy haircuts in a salon around the corner from our apartment. Because I knew French better than she, and Mark didn't speak it at all, I spoke for all of us—which I loved.

One evening we headed out near Versailles to the home of Francoise, my French friend who'd been part of our canoe trip in the summer. She prepared a beautiful three-course family dinner for us and her three grown children, all of whom we knew well, since each had spent summers with us in White Bear Lake. Christine, whom Mark had called "a twit" when she was thirteen, now cradled a baby. She had tears in her eyes as she slowly turned the pages of the photo album I'd brought. "He had so much energy," she said as I remembered how they'd fought like siblings for the best place in front of the television. That evening, especially after 9-11, I felt comforted by one big extended family unfettered by national borders.

Years earlier, our family had spent the month of August in Francoise's house while she and her family were on vacation. Peter was twelve, Ann was fourteen, and Lyn, nine. We used their Renault van to explore the environs, going to the Loire one weekend and making it to the Atlantic Coast near Saint Malo another. We even dipped our toes into the Mediterranean near St. Tropez. It was the family trip of a lifetime.

Now, in 2002, this romp through Paris tested the zeal we used to know for travel and adventure. No matter how hard we tried to enjoy ourselves—venturing into new neighborhoods and new shops, following Lyn wherever she wanted to go—our enthusiasm was muted. I was more interested in the people I knew than in the places. I wanted to make personal connections. The dinners with Francoise and her family, lunch with Lyn and her college roommate, and a night with Hans in Brussels pleased me more than monuments.

Hans, who is Swedish, had been our first international student. He lived with us for a year when he was seventeen—and Mark and I weren't much older—just after we had moved back to Minnesota. Hans spent his senior year at White Bear High School, cross-country skied, helped out around the house, and participated in the raising of our then-brood of one toddler and one infant.

When Lyn left us for London, we missed her. Mark and I continued to meander through the streets, gazing at the window displays, stopping at patisseries, but not even the *chaussons aux pommes* tasted as good as they once had. I was compelled to enter most every church we passed to look for the chapel of St. Peter's, and if I found one, I lit a candle for my Peter. I adored this ritual of lighting candles in memory of loved ones. Dropping euros in the coin box, I left a trail of sparkling candles for Peter throughout the city.

The few quiet dinners I had with Mark in bistros often brought me to tears. Our intimate table talk was still sad, and I passed on the wine, faithful to the pledge I'd made in the first days after Peter's death. Paris just didn't feel as romantic anymore.

I was immersed in memories of the earlier visit to Paris. I dredged up details of those first few days alone with the kids before Mark came, when Shelley and Bente, who were living in London, came to join us in Paris. It had been so hot that August. Peter wore soccer shorts and a T-shirt and we carried bottles of water we had frozen overnight in the freezer at Francoise's house. Peter was our leader, the only boy among three girls, and he and the girls waded in most every pool of water we came across. There are lots of pools in Paris.

At the grand plaza of the pyramid of the Louvre, Peter simply couldn't resist the tall new fountains, and all the kids took off their shoes and climbed over the low retaining walls to get to the fountain jets. Afterward, when it was time to go into the museum, Peter couldn't find a shoe. We looked and looked, even searched the garbage cans. Finally, he put a sock on one foot, a shoe on the other, and hobbled along, uncomplaining, until we bought him a pair of rubber soccer sandals on the Rue de Rivoli. Quite the scene!

On our whirlwind drive down to the south of France, we stopped briefly at Chartres to gaze up at the tall imposing stained glass windows, then barreled down the autoroute at breakneck speed to the sunny south. At the medieval fortress of Carcassonne we climbed the cobblestone pathways, explored the turreted towers, peered into torture chambers, and cheered at the reenactment of a jousting match.

We had dinner in a nearby village, and the three kids dared to try cuisine à la française. Ann ordered cassoulet with beans and duck and sausage, Peter, the rabbit, and Lyn, the pigeon. They cleaned their plates. Their faces dropped, however, and Peter groaned, when a little dog jumped down from the plump lap of an older lady at a nearby table and ate from a tiny bowl at her feet. Peter thought the French were pretty weird about their dogs.

Now, in March, while we were strolling one afternoon, Mark and I found ourselves in Montmartre, close to the basilica of Sacré Coeur, the pearly onion-domed cathedral dominating the Parisian skyline. We hadn't been inside since we took the kids there all those years earlier, and something told us to go in.

The interior was cavernous, dim with candle-light, nearly empty but for a few solemn worshippers in the pews and some wandering tourists. I walked to the center of the nave and looked up in awe at the towering dome, remembering how we had climbed to the top with the kids, and then recorded the number of steps in the back of the Michelin guidebook. I looked for the chapel of St. Peter, paused to light a candle, and said a prayer for Peter. An enormous sense of calm enveloped me.

On leaving the church, Mark and I both felt like we'd re-tread some holy steps. The cobblestones felt familiar under our feet. Ambling down the hill, we stopped near the patch of park where we had once pic-nicked on bread, cheese, and salami with our younger, more innocent fam-ily.

The following night, we had dinner with Bernard, one of Peter's co-workers from Deutsche Bank, one in the flood of black suits who had come through the line at the memorial service in Minnesota. I had been so astonished when he said, "I'm Bernard . . . from Paris," that I was tempted to run after him; I didn't know Peter had ever worked in Paris. I didn't know he had spent time with French co-workers. Peter had never wanted to meet up with us anywhere in France.

Over dinner that night Bernard told us he and Peter worked on many deals together in the bank's London office. Peter was brilliant, Bernard said, at crunching the numbers. Bernard described in great detail how he had gotten the news of Peter's death while at work in the Paris office. On the way home to his apartment in Montmartre, he had stopped in the basilica of Sacré Coeur. Devastated, he prayed for a while, he said. Peter had given one of his old ID cards to Bernard so he could let himself into the London office. At the basilica, Bernard slipped Peter's ID card between two chinks of stone in the wall and left it there in Peter's mem-ory. I thought of how holy we had felt in that church. Perhaps Peter's ID card was there still, near the chapel of St. Peter, near the spot where I had felt so peaceful.

We were elated a day later when Peter's flatmate, Mac, came from London by the chunnel, ostensibly on business but really to see us. We met him at Angelina's on the Rue de Rivoli, the same street Peter had trod in only one shoe after losing the other in the fountains of the Louvre. Sit-ting in a crowded corner of the touristy but classic teahouse, pouring thick-as-honey molten chocolate from pitchers and topping it with frothy whipped cream, we listened as Mac rambled about the grind of his work, his loneliness in London without Peter, his hopes of getting back to New York. He and Mark chided each other about their training for the AIDS bike ride from San Francisco to Los Angeles in June, and challenged each other to pick up the pace.

As he hugged us and said *au revoir*, Mac gave us detailed directions to the apartment on the Isle Saint Louis where he used to live in college, the site of the fabled scene that had made Peter resolve never to visit France again. Peter had forbidden his friends to ever tell us, or any of his high school friends who might tell us, but we had heard the story for the first time on the patio the night after his memorial service.

During the spring semester of their junior year, Mac was living in Paris while Peter was living in London. Other friends lived in Madrid, so they often met up in Paris at Mac's flat. One weekend night six or eight guys were out reveling in the warm Parisian spring air, wearing nothing but boxer shorts and wrapped in French flags—reckless youth showing a bit of disrespect. Very late, when they were very drunk, they headed back to Mac's apartment along the sleepy residential streets on the island behind Notre Dame, singing and swaying down the center of the narrow street. Someone, no one remembers who, zeroed in on the tiny Le Cars parked alongside the curb. One thing led to another, and soon they picked up one or two and placed them crosswise on the street, blocking all traffic. It wasn't long before they heard the sirens of the gendarme. They dashed to Mac's apartment and slammed the door behind them, yukking it up about their joke on the French.

Things quieted down and most of the guys drifted off to sleep, but Peter decided to take a look. He went to the door and opened it a crack. When he poked out his head, he was nabbed by the gendarme, hauled down to the local gendarmerie, and locked up for the rest of the night. Only when he rang the bell of the flat the next morning and woke up all the other guys, did they realize what had happened. Peter barged into the apartment, threw an official-looking piece of paper on the floor, and bellowed, "We're getting out of here!"

Their holiday sojourn to the French Alps was abruptly redirected to the Swiss Alps. And Peter swore to his friends he would never return to France—certain that if he did, he'd be immediately arrested. We finally understood why Peter hadn't wanted to visit Francoise or her family, and why he had declined to meet us in France. I couldn't help but wonder how he felt spending the night in a French prison cell. Peter's French wasn't great . . . He must have been afraid . . .

Now I could see some uncanny parallels to that night in Atlantic City. He was drunk, he was with friends, he was daring and did something no one else would do. He got caught and he got in trouble. What had impelled him? Did he take such chances purposefully? Did booze make him strong or stupid?

Maybe it was just youthful bravado? It could be easy to pass off the stories, to say, Oh well, boys will be boys. True enough, but his boldness in Atlantic City had gotten him killed.

Ten

First Anniversary

We sat around tables of eight at an event sponsored by our local children's hospital. Rabbi Harold Kushner, who wrote *When Bad Things Happen to Good People* after his son's death at age fourteen from progeria, or premature aging, expressed compassionate, heartfelt words to comfort us, all grieving parents. "It never helps to assign blame for our tragedies to God's will. God is crying too. God is with us, near us, ready to comfort us."

He said resenting someone who doesn't do or say the right thing in the face of another's tragedy rarely helps that person and only hurts the one who is grieving. Give it up, he told us.

I had often experienced the awkwardness of others. At one social gathering, when I entered the room, a woman stood and came over to me, looked me in the eye, and then said, "I can't deal with it." Another time someone asked me, "How are you doing?" but she walked off without a reply after I answered honestly, "It's difficult."

The most frequent comment was one that never made me feel better: "You are so courageous." I always wanted to shout back, "What choice do I have?"

One very good friend angered me when she said she had it all figured out. "It's just like police brutality—one guy going crazy." I thought her remark trivialized the death of my son, threw it into the category of all the other deaths by violence. Peter was unique, and *my* son, not a newspaper statistic, and I wished she had kept her assessments to herself.

Sometimes friends hovered too soliticitously, sticking to my side and making me feel helpless, as happened at a funeral when I was struggling to keep my composure. I hated being treated like an invalid. Luckily no one ever suggested aloud that Peter was in a "better place," or I might have bashed them.

It was maddening to have to deal with others' discomfort in our bereaved state, but I eventually accepted this as my responsibility—we have to guide others show their compassion in ways that help us. It's a matter of experience, I have learned. People who haven't been in this place do not know what to say or do. They intend to be compassionate, they mean well, and we must be frank about what we need.

Someone asked Rabbi Kushner about helping siblings cope with the death of a child. In answer, he cited a study in which 100 percent of parents said they paid extra attention to the sibling after the loss of a child, but that 100 percent of those siblings said they felt ignored. Both points of view are valid, he said. "You can't expect parents to do it all at a time of crisis." He wished he had assigned another family member to watch over his daughter when his son died, he said.

I thought about the care with which we thought we had tended our daughters after Peter's death. I thought about how they were both present in the house during that awful week but still felt distant. I thought about Charlie, who was hovering over me as well as taking care of the girls. Bless my friend, but did anyone worry about my daughters enough? Probably no one could have really taken the place of their parents at the time of their brother's death, or even later, and now I regret that I was too often turned in on myself and oblivious to their needs. Yet, if it all happened over again, I'd probably make the same mistake.

At the end of his comments, I approached the rabbi and asked him about losing a son to homicide. He said little other than that we must feel resentful. It was too early in our grief, he said, for us to expect to feel anything else. He said he would want revenge and justice, and he too would probably want to attend the trial. He was kind but cool, and I left with the sense he didn't know much about losing a child to murder.

Nevertheless, the evening made an impact. Afterward I heard Mark mention several times to friends the rabbi's suggestion of thinking about the legacy of our son's life and thinking of ourselves as living out the unlived years of our child's life as fully and as meaningfully as possible in tribute to the memory of our child. We both had gained hope . . . and renewed purpose.

But purpose was illusory these days. Without a job, a sense of purpose would be my nemesis. What would I do? How would I keep myself occupied? Focused? Content? I had always taken myself so seriously. I was worried I'd fall apart without an imposed routine.

I was afraid of being alone. Having such a feeble grasp on the treacherous road of grief, I feared I would sink irretrievably into the pit of despair. I saw myself hugging the sides of a well shaft, reaching, climbing and kicking, yet unable to reach the light at the top of the well. The light, I knew at some level, was my faith that God was with me and would not abandon me, but I was not yet convinced.

First, I had to face my fears of being alone. To immerse myself in my own company, I headed to an Episcopal retreat center, the House of Prayer, a couple hours' drive from the Twin Cities. I took my journal, my Bible, some family photo albums, and a few favorite books about child loss: Ann Weems's *Psalms of Lament*; Nicholas Wolterstorff's *Lament for a Son*; Anne McCracken and Mary Semel's *A Broken Heart Still Beats*. I also packed the loose-leaf binder I'd assembled of news articles about Peter's death and some of the hundreds of notes we'd received.

I was alone with my grief. In my tidy, simple cell, I opened the floodgate to my tears, my anxieties, my sadness. I wallowed day and night in remembrances of Peter. I cried. I prayed.

Late one afternoon I walked to the nearby abbey at St. John's University to sit in the sanctuary for a change of scenery and to absorb the beauty of the chapel. It was coincidentally prayer time, so priests and monks gradually began to file into their places behind the altar. One man in street clothes came up to me in the pews and invited me to join the monks up front. I was reluctant, but he persisted and led me up the side aisle to a wooden booth in the chancel, handing me a big book, and pointing out their place in the liturgy of the day's worship service. I simply acquiesced . . . and allowed myself to be enveloped in God's love. The melodious chords of the chanting coursed through the chambers of my broken heart, touched the painful places, smoothed salve on wounds I was helpless to heal.

In my journal, I wrote: *I sense a few sutures pulling and tugging around my heart. I feel myself standing on a ledge near the top of the pit, peering*

up to the light beyond the well shaft. I'm calm though I'm still several lengths
below the rim of the pit. Maybe I can lift my body a bit higher, raise up my arm,
reach farther . . . by your power, O God.

I knew I was struggling to acknowledge that Peter was indeed dead. In my brain, I knew I would never be able to feel his hug again or smell his clothes or see the twinkle in his eye. But I felt him with me constantly . . . physically . . . in his body. I saw him at eight years old on the neighbor's bike, at age twelve on the tennis court. I saw him water-skiing, the rope's handle crooked in his elbow, all grace and strength. I saw his back heading into the airport terminal, his suit bag over his shoulder, on the day he left for Atlantic City.

He would always be with me. Yes, I would try to be like Peter, for what better way was there to try to live out the unlived years of his life, to carry forward his legacy. I was resigned to carrying sorrow forever, but I would try to carry gratitude as well.

On my knees in the tiny octagonal meditation chapel at the retreat center, alone in the light of the candles, I finally acknowledged my simmering anger. I was terrified of its power to overwhelm me. I was tempted to blame God . . . but then who would bear me up? I could target all the friends and acquaintances who made callous comments, but I needed the compassion they also offered. I could sling my arrows at Peter's friends who were partly responsible for getting him to Atlantic City, but I couldn't bear to lose that connection to Peter.

I had so many questions. Why did the altercation happen? Why did all the bouncers fight only Peter? What was he doing at the club until four? How drunk was he? How did they knock him down? Did they mean to kill him? Why? Why did they abandon him on the street? Where were his clothes? His wallet? His credit card? What were his last words to his friends?

And I was angry. But that was all right. Anger, I decided, was a legitimate feeling—a bona fide emotion somewhere on the other side of joy and delight, one I used to be uncomfortable with. But since Peter's death, anger, like sadness and gratitude, had became part of me. It felt good to let off a little steam—to rant and rave. Like a pressure cooker that spouts when it gets too hot, an outburst of anger enabled me to simmer down, forgive others, and forgive myself.

I was angry at God for not protecting Peter. Yet time and time again, Linda, my preacher and friend Linda, told me God could take that blame. I was angry at the murderer for his uncontrolled rage. I was angry at the other bouncers who let it happen and then participated. I was even angry with Peter for his fateful choices. But there was no resolution for that anger, no way to explain it away. It happened. Anger or no anger, nothing could be fixed. Linda suggested I try to express my anger lightly and calmly before it exploded into rage in a hurtful way. I wasn't sure I knew how to do that.

At the end of my retreat, I felt more at peace. I faced the pain, the emptiness, and I touched the anger. I felt ready to leave the abbey, to go home to live in the sunshine, to walk and be in my garden. I was no longer afraid of my days at home alone. I saw an opportunity to become my own best friend. I felt assured I would continue to live and I knew Peter would live with me always.

Peter, twenty-two, on Mark's birthday.

I didn't feel lonely. In my backyard, the sun shone on my face. The blaze of the sun felt like the light of God. He knows me, I told myself. He bears my aches, comforts me, and walks with me. I finally grasped the difference between solitude and loneliness. Earl Grollman wrote, "Solitude is not loneliness; loneliness is the pain of being alone. Solitude is the glory of being alive." I would never be alone, for I had been invited to walk with God on this journey. I needed only to seize his hand.

THE FIRST ANNIVERSARY OF PETER'S death was obsessing me. How would we celebrate it or mark it or mourn it? Lyn would not be home, preferring to stay at camp with friends. Though I'd miss her, I realized the woods of northern Minnesota adorned the sanctuary in which she felt closest to her brother.

Mark's birthdays and mine were a week apart in mid-June. Even our birthdays were difficult during that first year of firsts after Peter's death. On my birthday I kept staring at the last birthday gift I'd gotten from Peter just a few days before his death—a camp-sized espresso maker intended to keep me happy on the impending canoe trip. It sat on the kitchen counter for a year, right next to a birthday card from him showing a kid on the front hugging his mom and on the inside: "Mom, remember all of the aggravation I used to cause you?" When I opened the card, it read, "I'm almost done."

On his birthday, Mark seemed sullen and said little. We rode our bikes twenty-five miles in the morning, and then sat around for the rest of the afternoon. When the girls called in late afternoon, his spirits lifted. They chatted lightheartedly and I noted with pleasure how they tried to take care of him. All day long, however, I harbored hope that one of Peter's friends might call too, though I knew it was unrealistic. They had their own fathers; they didn't need to think about Mark.

At the end of the day, Mark summed it up. "It's you and me now, Mary." Sad, but profoundly true. With our daughters away from the nest and getting on with their lives, and with one child gone forever, we would have to bind our own wounds and take care of each other.

The morning of the summer solstice, I rose before dawn and headed to the golf course, eager to experience every minute of the longest day of the year. Walking the course backward from the eighteenth hole, as was my habit, I thought about grief. In the half-light of half-sanity before sunrise, my grief felt like an abstraction, a bundle with its own identity, shape, and weight. Heavy and dark, nothing like Peter.

A few days before a friend had told me, "I keep thinking of Peter. For some reason, Mary, I think he's worried about you."

And I couldn't help thinking, What would Peter want? I was suddenly willing to consider that by paying too much attention to this mysterious, ugly, misshapen blob of grief, I was doing an injustice to the memory of my handsome, broad-shouldered, big-handed son. He was what I wanted to hold in my heart, not the concept of grief. But how would I ever separate the one from the other?

For months I had envisioned a big gathering on the anniversary, July 8, our friends encircling us on the patio, maybe a golf event and a bike ride, a late-evening bonfire with Peter's friends coming too. On some level, I thought the more people and the more fun, the more likely Peter would come too. I had even drafted an elaborate e-mail invitation when Mark said, "It's not a goddamn party, Mary." He was right, of course. It was not the time to recruit, to lure, folks to come to hold our hands.

On Sunday, July 7, a huge arrangement of yellow sunflowers and orange roses we'd ordered for the church altar glowed from the communion table. During the processional, Darlene winked at us, and then she preached about Celtic Christianity and the "thin places"—moments or places where the veil separating heaven and earth appears transparent and we feel especially close to those we have lost. She chose "For the Beauty of the Earth," perhaps because it was the hymn we'd sung at Peter's memorial service. Mark and I felt loved.

Without invitation, people visited us all day Sunday and all day the next. Our house filled with flowers, including some from Peter's friends in the East. Early in the evening, about the same time Peter had dined with friends at the Tun Tavern the year before, on the final day of his life, a couple dozen friends of ours and of our kids gathered on the hillside next to the lake.

"You need us, and we're here for you," one said. "We'll all have our time of need." Another said, "We all lost something with the death of Peter."

We grabbed hands and made a huge circle around a small but sturdy burr oak tree Lyn had helped us purchase and Mark and Ann had planted that afternoon. Our friend Kris read a poem about a leaf flitting from tree to tree in autumn, like Peter visiting all of us since his death, and then she asked for a moment of silence.

Among our friends, we felt cared for and cherished.

As we lingered over a bonfire at the lake, I considered the day not only a memorial to Peter but a celebration of our family. Though broken—we were all right. We had survived one year.

Monday morning, July 8, Mark, Ann and I got up early, threw on fleece, and trudged down to the dock to sit, for Peter, from four to five o'-clock. The mother of one of Peter's high school friends was already on the bench with a thermos of coffee and a bag of doughnuts. Silently we sat together in the gentle rain, gazing at the still water, soaking up the peace in the soft warm mist. The rain felt like heaven's tears.

When our family—except for Lyn, who had stayed at camp—was alone again in the evening, Ann and I walked down to the dock. The night was calm, full of stars—and mosquitoes. We each lit little candles for Peter and set them afloat on the water beside the dock, watching them hover on the surface of the water near us. By the light of the candles and stars, we began to tear apart fading bouquets of flowers sent to mark the anniversary and tossed the remnant blossoms into the water. With each tossing we called out in turn: "This is for your big feet. This one is for your gray hairs. This one is for the birthmark on the side of your body. This one is for your mathematical genius. This one is for your friends." Then we shouted, "We love you Peter!" We asked him to stay close to us, to show us signs, to help us. Then we ran like hell back to the house to escape the mosquitoes!

I wished the calm could have lasted. I wished I could have stayed in the joy of Peter's life. Embraced by friends, we relished remembering a son and brother who had lived. Afterward, alone again, the pain of remembering that he had died was so much sharper.

Eleven
Preparing for Trial

The trial for Peter's murder loomed. . . . It would begin in less than a month. I was girding my emotions. Our circle of supportive friends had grown noticeably smaller, and we felt isolated, even lonely. I suspected many people had no clue of what we were facing, even though I almost always referred to the trial when someone asked how we were. I thought about it constantly.

One question always lingered: "Why go if it's going to be so tough?" But I couldn't imagine not going. Going might be my final opportunity to be Peter's mom. I had to be there for Peter's sake.

Margaret was a mom whose twenty-four-year-old daughter, Kiersa, had been brutally raped and murdered a few years before. Her killer was on death row in Texas. Margaret and her husband and two surviving teenaged daughters had endured two weeks of trial and a third week of penalty phase. Margaret adopted me, and, with her unorthodox sense of humor somehow still intact, she helped me picture the tiny courtroom, the bailiff and the parade of officers with guns at their waist, the uncomfortable wooden benches, the anguish my family would face.

She described the tension we'd feel in the courtroom and the boredom of the long breaks between sessions. She suggested we try to walk every day, drink lots of water, and eat decent meals even though we wouldn't feel like eating. "Don't talk to reporters," she advised. "And watch out for them even in the bathrooms."

Mini-golf at the bachelor party in Atlantic City.

"And be sure to address the defendant with victim-impact state-ments when you get the chance," she said. "It was our chance to express pent-up emotion."

I had no idea what I'd tell the defendant in our case. Would I tell him he had ruined our lives?

ONE MORNING BEFORE WORK, Mark and I met with a friend from church, a judge who had recently presided over a murder trial in St. Paul. The vic-tim was an eighteen-year-old who had been riding his bike home after work late one night when he was gunned down by a passing carload of alleged gang members. "What will it feel like to sit through a murder trial?" I asked him. "How do we get prepared?"

Our friend the judge told us the family of the cyclist was present whenever the jury was in the courtroom. "The presense of the family can make the deceased person come alive for the jury." From that moment on, Mark never mentioned again not attending the trial.

"It's not going to be easy," the judge said. "You'll want to stay in the most comfortable place you can find so you can relax when you're not in the courtroom."

He too predicted members of the press would be present and asking for comments. "In my experience, it rarely helps to make comments. The reporters are not really interested in you or Peter, just in selling newspapers."

He scared us when he said we might be called on to testify. Though we hadn't witnessed Peter's murder, the prosecutor might want us to make the victim real, to speak for the son who couldn't speak for himself.

"Don't forget, whatever the outcome, it's not going to bring Peter back."

Then he asked what we would do after the trial, that we should expect a period of letdown. My stomach turned, my muscles tensed. I couldn't imagine feeling worse. In that moment, I decided to accept a new job I'd been offered at a nonprofit publishing company. It sounded like the plan I needed for after the trial.

"How likely is a plea negotiation before the start of the trial?" the judge asked.

Mark nodded his head. "It's what I've been praying for. Anything to avoid going to trial," he said. "I'd gladly accept the defendant's plea to a lesser charge if it would avert a trial, but so far he hasn't shown the slightest interest in any deal."

"Well, just remember that a negotiated plea is better than going to trial. A trial is bound to get really ugly. The defense will consistently try to paint the victim in the worst possible light, cast blame on the behavior of your son and doubt on Pete Steinberg's testimony. The closer you get to the start date of the trial, the more likely a plea bargain. Usually the most intense negotiations occur just before the start of the trial, because the defense waits until the last possible moment in order to cut the best deal."

I couldn't believe my ears. After thirteen months of waiting, we could possibly not have a trial? Suddenly I realized how much I had invested in the prospect of a trial, how desperately I wanted one. I realized I was counting on hearing about my son, going over the details of his final day, seeing his friends, hearing his name. . . . Yes, I was counting on keeping him alive. I knew then I wasn't prepared for any trial, or for any outcome. And I knew I certainly was not prepared for life *after* a trial.

The prosecutor had previewed his case with us over several long phone conversations. We heard about the body, the blows, the cause of death, and whether the defendant intended to cause "probable" or "possible" death. The prosecutor's job was to be pragmatic and analytical, not to respond to the emotions of the family. He was paid by the state, not by us. This was the State of New Jersey against Tamer Shahid. We had very little influence.

I was offended by his cold calculations, which seemed to disregard our—Peter's—humanity. I decided I would have to be the image lady—the one during the trial responsible for reminding everyone that Peter was a living, loving, flesh-and-blood human being. I would make this trial about more than a dead body. I would find a way to be the sparkle and the strength of my son, Peter.

In the mornings after showering, as I dried and brushed my hair, I couldn't help but pat the back of my head, the spot where Peter had been kicked, I'd heard, over and over again, even when he was unconscious, where he had bled to death even though there wasn't a drop of blood on his scalp. This spot on my head, I said to myself. Such a fragile spot.

FINALLY, I DECIDED I NEEDED TO COME OUT of my cocoon. I needed to face every fact about that final day of Peter's life in Atlantic City. So far I hadn't wanted to know the details of his attack, his injuries, how exactly he died. I had been clinging to his life, by denying his death. But the trial would be all about his death. I didn't want to be surprised in the courtroom by something I could have known about in advance. The surprises could undo me.

I arranged a conference call with Chris and Robby, friends of Peter who were at the bachelor party, who'd offered many times to answer our questions, and I prepared a list of what I wanted to ask them. In front of me I laid the photos the groom had given us of their afternoon and evening in Atlantic City. I began by asking first about the evening before the party and then about the day of the party in order to work up my courage to hearing about the awful night.

"Who decided on Atlantic City? Why?"

"I did," replied Chris, the best man. "It was centrally located and sounded like a fun place. None of us had been there before."

"When did Peter get there?"

"He drove in from Philadelphia with Steinberg about nine on Friday night. We were watching the baseball game in our room. When the game ended, Peter and a few guys went to the casino next door. They played a little keno. It wasn't especially late when they came back and went to bed."

"What did you do all day Saturday?

"We got up late and strolled along the boardwalk. It took us awhile to review the options for lunch. We wound up with what I'd call a pretty bad lunch at Hooters," Chris said. "After lunch, some of the guys went to the beach while Peter went with some others to play go-carts. I remember he had a two-seater to himself and tried to be the fastest. He was the fastest. Of course, we told him it was just because he had the better car."

I gazed at the photo in front of me of Peter in the red go-cart, knees up to his chest, smirk on his face, looking like a big overgrown kid.

"Then we went to play mini-golf." I looked at another photo: Peter in a line of six guys, his hands on the club, bare feet lined up, pretending to putt. Everyone was smiling, their arms wrapped around each other's shoulders.

After mini-golf the group split up, Chris and Robby said. A few of the guys went to the beach, and the others went to the casinos. They regrouped at the hotel late in the afternoon to get dressed for seven o'clock dinner reservations at the Tun Tavern, a couple blocks from their hotel. They walked, as they had all day, because they knew they'd be drinking.

One photo shows a dozen young men in buttoned-down shirts seated around a large table. Later, during the trial, the judge would comment on this photo and admit it as evidence since it showed just one pitcher of beer on the table, substantiating, he said, the fairly sober and responsible character of the group.

"And what happened afterward?" I boldly asked, finally finding the courage to deal with the last hours of my son's life.

"Steinberg and Westra went back to the hotel and asked the concierge where we could go to continue our party. The concierge suggested the second-floor VIP room at the Naked City, just a couple blocks away. So Steinberg and Westra reserved the room from 11:15 until 1:15. For forty dollars per person, we got our own space, all we could drink, dancers, and our own waiters."

And your own bouncers, I thought.

"When the open bar closed," Chris said, "the guys gradually drifted off to their hotel rooms and went to bed. When I left about three

I thought it had been a pretty good night. There were just three guys left in the bar then—Westra, Steinberg, and Greg."

Then he murmured, "I've asked myself so many times since if there were any flashpoints of violence during the evening. But I'm certain I didn't see anything. I just remember seeing Peter and Shahid, the bouncer, talking to each other in the VIP room. They seemed friendly, easygoing, no loud words."

The next thing Chris knew—at eight on Sunday morning, July 8—Pete Steinberg came back to the hotel with a policeman. The policeman stayed in the hallway while Steinberg wokeup his friends, told them Westra had been attacked, and told them he had died.

I shuddered when I heard that. In my bones I felt so sorry for those guys in the hotel that morning. How their lives were changed in that moment.

The policeman wanted a statement from Greg, who had been sitting at the VIP bar, his back to the action, when Shahid hauled Westra down the stairs. Steinberg saw what was happening, so he followed, but Greg was oblivious. He had heard nothing, he knew nothing. When police arrived and closed the club, Greg gave his name to the officers like all the other patrons, left past the yellow tape marking the scene from which the victim had already been removed, and went back to his hotel to bed. He had no idea his friend was the victim until Steinberg and the policeman came to the hotel.

"Was Peter drunk?" I asked.

"We had all been drinking," Chris and Robby said. "But no, Westra was not inordinately drunk."

I hesitated, took a deep breath, and then asked the question I'd been trying to ask out loud for months. "Did either of you see Peter groping the dancers like the newspapers said? Please . . . tell me the truth."

"No. We didn't see Peter groping the dancers," they both said.

I believed them.

To BRACE OURSELVES FOR THE TRIAL, Mark and I retreated at the end of July with our friends Kris and Gerry to a ranch in Wyoming, one they'd been going to for years, where they promised we'd have space for solace and reflection before the trial. Mark and I took our time driving west along the route Lewis and Clark had crisscrossed, and we listened to *Un-*

daunted Courage, the chronicle of their journey. We saw the same bluffs and the same streams as the explorers. We passed a state park named for a Mandan chief, and at almost the same moment we listened on CD to how the chief had helped the two explorers. At Dubois, we turned off the highway and headed up into the dry hills of Wyoming, the countryside growing greener and more beautiful with every mile. Ospreys circled in flight. A trout stream percolated down the valley. Then the ranch peeked out from behind the pines, and we saw the log cabins nestled in the folds of grass and rocks beside the stream. We both teared up at the placid scene of towering trees, distant mountains, horses grazing in the fields. Peter should be able to see this, I thought. We'll never be able to bring him to this ranch. It wasn't fair.

We settled into our tiny log cabin, went for horseback rides into high mountain valleys blazing with blue lupine, walked and watched birds, and practiced our nascent fly-fishing skills under Gerry's tutelage. We read books, retired early, and slept deeply until awakened by the clang of the breakfast bell that beckoned us to a hearty home-cooked meal in the lodgepole pine dining room.

I was looking for Peter everywhere. With peace and quiet and the beauty of nature surrounding me, he just had to be present. I sat on the porch of our cabin, stared beyond the pastures to the majestic craggy bluffs, cast my eye on Hole in the Wall, a weathered window of granite, and begged for signs of Peter's presence. I finally found him in the light breeze tickling the tops of the pine trees, ever so subtle, yet ever so present. Brush my face, breeze, brush my face, I implored.

And I found him again in his father, my husband, Mark. I watched Mark head off in waders across the pasture, fishing rod in hand, walking next to Gerry and eager to practice his newfound sport, and I'd lovingly think of how everything I have left of Peter is in this man.

Peter would want me to take care of his father—to love him enough for the both of us. But it was more than that. I would cherish him. The father was the son, and the son was the father. The two were made of nearly the same molecules, had the same bounce in their gait, the same glint in their eye, the same soft smiles.

Now Mark and I had only each other. We were each other's best friend in our remembrance of the unforgettable. Peter was the offspring of the two of us, a bit of Mark and a bit of me. He continued to take life from our hopes and dreams and memories. Together, as mother and father, our son would be our future as well as our past.

At the ranch I dared to contemplate the huge concepts that had been prickling the walls of my fragile heart. Evil. I could scarcely grasp it, but it plagued me. How would I prepare myself to meet evil people, to protect myself, and to protect my loved ones?

It was so much easier to think of unlucky Pete, buried on Friday, July 13. It was so much easier to think of his death as an unlucky coincidence, something that could have happened to any of the guys at the bachelor party that night, just like the groom's mother told me after Peter's memorial service. "I'm just so sorry it was *your* son."

I desperately wanted to understand. I needed to understand, intellectually as well as emotionally, why my son was killed. There must be laws against roughing up patrons, beating them until they lost consciousness. And attacking on the pavement outside the door of the club! Isn't that public space beyond their jurisdiction?

I wanted justice. It was wrong, woefully wrong, that my son was killed by a bouncer outside a club. How could Peter's behavior possibly have warranted such a drubbing? Even if he had groped the dancers, which I didn't believe, how could such a transgression—in a strip club—earn him a forcible eviction from the VIP room, a beating outside by bouncers, the bar's owner, and the bar's manager? Why would Shahid kick him in the head over and over again unless he meant to inflict mortal damage?

Shahid must be evil. He must have wanted to kill my son.

I knew deep down we'd never right the injustice, for Peter would not come alive again. But we were definitely seeking retribution. I knew the risk of not moving past our anger and resentment was real, probably one reason I had been so slow to even acknowledge my anger. I suspected we might feel shortchanged and deprived even after a trial. I was even afraid we might become depraved—angry and bitter forever. And I knew a stone-cold distance, like death itself, could grow in the spaces left after the trial, among us, our beloved daughters, and friends. Even between Mark and me.

Why Peter died, I already suspected, didn't really matter. The villain kicked him repeatedly and now my son was dead. So many efforts to explain, to give meaning to, to understand what happened made me furious. It was like grasping at straws: Peter went to a bad place. He drank. He got into a fight. So what? Trying to understand why Peter died made me feel awful.

In my heart, I knew I'd never be satisfied. How could any explanation justify what Peter got: precious life knocked out of his vigorous twenty-four-year-old hunk of a body, left dead on the pavement. It wasn't easy for me to acknowledge the presence of evil in my life. But I had no other word for what had killed my son.

Now, I see how my vision of things was polarized during those months. I felt more secure, then, looking through absolutes, infallibles, rights and wrongs. It would have overwhelmed me to consider the shades of gray that lay in irresponsibility, happenstance, loyalty, hazard. I couldn't cope with ambiguity.

I was treading unknown territory, and I was afraid. My head was ruled by my heart.

Peter skiing with workmates in February 2001.

Twelve
Trial

It was like driving into hell with no way of turning back, no hope of coming out unscathed. The Atlantic City Parkway was lined with orchards and green fields, but its billboards splashed with scantily clad girls advertising gambling and fun, fun, fun, sickened us. Our exit came none too soon. As we exited the freeway on the western edge of Atlantic County, the misty shadowed towers of tall casino hotels loomed on the distant northeastern horizon

I hoped and prayed I would remain strong for my son. I didn't have to look at the perpetrator, I decided. I didn't have to meet his eye. I would think about Peter, not Shahid. I would maintain my son's dignity as well as my own. I wanted my son, even in death, to be proud of his mother.

In downtown Mays Landing, the county seat of Atlantic County, we met Jackie, the victim witness coordinator, with whom we'd often talked by phone. She had helped us find our condo in nearby Ocean City and now she felt like a friend as she took us to meet the prosecutor. She led us away from the chunky, imposing Carnegie Library-style courthouse and took us instead across the street to a plain, one-story commercial building. It was Sunday, so she unlocked the front door and then led us down a narrow corridor to a chaotic workroom, where Murray, the prosecutor, was sitting in blue jeans and golf shirt at a table cluttered with papers.

He was soft-spoken, short, thin, nearly our age—nothing like what I had expected from the formal, lawyerly voice we'd gotten to know

on the phone. Was this the man who would confront the slimebags of Atlantic City casinos and strip clubs? Was this the man who would establish
blame and bring us justice? With few words, he greeted us, and then pulled
up a couple folding chairs and began to talk about the case, step by step,
in a formal, slightly aloof, but polite tone of voice. He didn't show much
emotion, and he didn't seem very compassionate about our loss. It was
business to him. It wasn't his son.

Murray ran us through a list of mundane questions about Peter's
childhood illnesses and athletic accidents and medical treatments. Did he
have any surgeries? Was he ever sick? Was he injured in sports? Did he
ever experience a head injury? He listed the witnesses he planned to call,
the facts he'd present, the case he intended to build. We would not be expected to testify, he told us, because we hadn't been present at the scene
of the crime. As he droned on, I felt like I was being interviewed by a television newsman. I felt detached from my son.

From my backpack I pulled out two framed photos of Peter and
set them on the table in front of Murray. "This is Peter," I said. "This is
who was beaten to death." He glanced at the photos but didn't say anything. Still I persisted in my efforts to personalize the dead body, pulling
out a T-shirt from the Middlebury memorial hike and offering it to him.
He seemed slightly embarrassed to take the shirt with Peter's name on it,
but he asked about the bear on the back of the shirt, among friends, watching the sunset over the Green Mountains. I told him how Peter, coming
from White Bear Lake, had adopted the polar bear as his mascot.

After about an hour of questions, when it was time to go, I packed
up my framed photos, but I left Murray with an envelope of additional
photos including the ones the groom had taken the day Peter died, the
ones of the go-carts and the dinner at the Tun Tavern. I left wondering
if he really knew enough about Peter to begin trial in two days. Didn't he
need anything more from us?

Jackie drove us back to our condo along brushy stretches of almost rural countryside in the environs of Atlantic City. "It's flat, just like
South Florida," she said. When we weren't traveling two-lane secondary
roads, we seemed stuck between stop lights on concrete strips bordered
by rundown motels, convenience stores, and fast food restaurants.

Only later, when I read about the bodies of four alleged prostitutes
dumped on the pike between the courthouse and our condo, would I grasp

the reality of the cesspool we'd broached. Thirty-four million tourists came each year to the faded resort city, where gambling had been legal for more than twenty-five years. More than one of our friends would tell us about signs on the insides of motel-room doors warning patrons not to go out on the streets at night. Shimmering casinos flourished along the boardwalk, but a thriving underground economy of sex and drugs and crime lurked in the shadows and stretched tentacles into neighboring communities. I'd never felt so far away from the lush green shores of White Bear Lake.

Jury selection filled the next day. Murray said it would be perfunctory and we need not attend. So we scouted the neighborhood of our condo and tried to get comfortable while we waited for our daughters to arrive. But comfort eluded us. It was agonizing to be so near to the scene of Peter's death. Everything felt strange, seedy, wrong.

Maybe I was naïve too, used to being sheltered and coddled just like the young men at the bachelor party were. I wanted to get the hell out of there. I couldn't shrug off the sense that Peter would be mortified we had to come to this place on his behalf to endure this trial.

IN MY JOURNAL, I WROTE: *Please don't cry, Peter. Nothing, nothing, nothing will diminish our love and pride in and for you. Nothing! Not the facts, not the bruised knuckles, not the blood-alcohol level. You did nothing wrong, nothing of which we are ashamed. You always were and always will be everything any parent could want in a son.*

ON AUGUST 13, 2002, MARK AND I, Ann, and Lyn arrived at the courthouse before the jury was sworn in. Jackie led us to the front of the small courtroom next to the railing just behind the prosecutor. Mark and I sat with the girls between us, Jackie one seat away, and the girls' closest friends in a row behind us. Soon our side of the courtroom was filled with friends from Minnesota, Pete Steinberg and his parents, and several Middlebury friends. On the defendant's side of the courtroom there were only a couple men in T-shirts.

I gave a laminated photo of Peter skiing with his work colleagues to everyone who came to support us. While we listened to gruesome details about his dead body, I wanted us to remember a living, loving Peter Westra. I wore a tiny silver-framed photo pin on my lapel until Jackie told me it wasn't a good idea. In another case, a photo worn by a family member had caused a mistrial. I immediately re-pinned the photo on the shirt under my jacket.

We listened as if through a fog to the prosecutor laying out his case, telling the court over and over again in so many different ways about this group of young Middlebury classmates who had come together for a weekend to celebrate the wedding of a friend and how tragically it had concluded. Chris, the best man who had planned the party, was the first witness to be called. He repeated what he had told me on the phone, saying they had decided to meet in a tourist town none of them had ever been to before because it was convenient and because they wanted to be together and to have fun.

"It was centrally located," Chris said so softly we could hardly hear him. "The guys were coming from Philadelphia, DC, Boston, Florida, New York and London. It was close to a major airport and offered activities and a beach we thought we'd enjoy." He looked so clean cut, so young.

"Did you come for the gambling?" Murray asked.

"No," said Chris. "Gambling wasn't the major reason."

Brad, the groom, took the stand. He looked scared. "Had you ever been to Atlantic City before that weekend?" Murray asked.

"No," Brad replied.

"What did you think?" Murray asked.

"We were a little surprised by the place. There was a lot of hawking on the boardwalk. It was a little sleazier than we expected."

Then Greg took the stand. He said he was sitting at the bar talking to the bartender, totally unaware of anything going on behind him. He said their group had been a bit ridiculed by the staff at the Naked City for being a lame bunch—not drinking much and not buying many lap dances. He told of leaving the club after police closed it, stepping through the yellow police tape without knowing what had happened, and then being awakened in the morning to find out his friend was dead.

The innocence of those boys, I thought. They were so green and good-looking, with wide-open faces, scrubbed and shorn, speaking softly but clearly, subdued. They were weekend tourists out of their element, sophisticated but ignorant, uncomfortable in a trashy environment, but wanting to enjoy each other's company. How quickly their innocence was quashed when one of them was killed.

How I clung to their innocence.

By the third day of the trial, when Pete Steinberg was scheduled to testify, every seat on our side of the courtroom was occupied. More than a dozen of his Middlebury friends had come to support him. He wore a blue oxford-cloth shirt and blue blazer like the other guys who'd testified, but he added a bright red tie with bicycles on it, chosen, he said, in tribute to Peter. He looked every bit the slightly nerdy, super-intelligent med school student. And he was stunningly articulate.

The other side of the aisle was now occupied by half a dozen men in shiny black suits, a couple women in the back rows, a few reporters, and a lawyer for the casinos. Directly behind the defendant sat a Coptic priest dressed in a long black gown, who from time to time held up a big shiny cross on a heavy chain and peered through its hole at witnesses.

Steinberg described how he was hanging out with Peter Westra in the upstairs VIP room at the Naked City long after the others, except Greg, had gone back to the hotel. Steinberg was sitting at the bar, nursing a beer, at about four in the morning when he noticed Westra talking to a bouncer just a few feet away.

"What were they doing?" Murray asked.

"They were talking to each other," Steinberg replied.

"How were they talking to each other?"

"They were chatting amiably, in a friendly manner."

"Did you overhear the conversation? Were they talking loudly?"

"No, I couldn't hear what they were saying. They seemed friendly with each other."

"And how far away from them were you?"

"Just a few feet. Maybe ten feet."

"What did you see next?" the prosecutor asked.

"I saw Westra put his hand on the bouncer's shoulder. Then, suddenly, the bouncer put Westra in an armlock and hauled him down the stairs. I didn't know what was going on."

"What did you do?"

"I followed them down the stairs."

"And what did you see outside?"

"I saw the bouncer throw Westra onto the hood of a Honda parked there, punch him several times."

"Did Westra fight back?"

"He returned a couple wild blows. Then the bouncer turned and went back into the bar."

"What happened next?"

"Westra was angry," Steinberg said. "He wanted to go back into the bar. I tried to get him to just go home, but he headed to the door. Maybe he wanted to get Greg, who was still upstairs at the bar, or maybe he wanted his credit card. I don't know why. Peter was bigger than me. He was drunk. I couldn't stop him from going back. When he tried to reenter, he was met by a wall of bouncers, knocked to the pavement, and kicked by all five of them."

Barely revealing emotion and in great command of every painstaking detail, Steinberg continued to testify that he too was knocked to the pavement, but not attacked. Peter alone seemed to be the target. Steinberg crawled on the pavement to put his body over Peter's head, to try to ward off the kicks. He showed two sketches he had made, one immediately after the attack and the other a couple days later, indicating the positions of five men around Peter's unconscious body: two on the right side, two on the left side, kicking him along his torso. But Steinberg was adamant that only one man was standing at Peter's head, repeatedly kicking him on the top of his head and in the back of his neck.

"He continued to kick him soccer-style on the crown of his head . . . yes, in the manner you would kick a football or a soccer ball," he said calmly.

"Do you see this man in the courtroom?" Murray asked.

"Yes, I do. That's him." And he pointed resolutely to Shahid.

I was shuddering, sick in every pore of my body hearing Pete Steinberg talk about crawling on the ground, putting his body over my son's head.

"Westra didn't move," he said.

I don't think he dared to let down. Not then, not when he was on the stand. He knew the case depended on his testimony. He didn't want to screw anything up.

Pete Steinberg said the attackers went back into the bar, leaving Westra on the pavement. Steinberg started CPR. A third-year med student, he knew exactly how to administer CPR in a manner that wouldn't cause further brain damage. Then he hailed a passing patrol car, exhorted the patrolman to call the paramedics, and even suggested a specific treatment once Peter arrived at the hospital.

"Did you go to the hospital with your friend?" Murray asked.

"No. They wouldn't let me go."

"But you knew your friend was pretty seriously injured, didn't you? You knew he might not make it."

"Yeah, I knew he probably wouldn't make it."

"How did you know?"

"I saw the V-fib on the monitor. That's not good."

"Did anyone ever tell you your friend had died?"

"No, no one ever told me."

Steinberg put me, put us all, on the sidewalk in front of the Naked City. I was on the hood of the Honda myself, on the pavement, the boots coming at me. I could feel Pete Steinberg's anguish as he crawled across the cement, trying to get to his friend, trying to protect his friend's head. He tried to save Peter's life. He tried, but he failed. I felt so sorry for him. Yet I was so grateful. I wanted to take care of him forever.

UNDER CROSS-EXAMINATION, Steinberg seemed to be the one on trial. How much had he had to drink? Was he drunk? Could he really see much from his spot on the pavement? Did he know what he was doing when he administered CPR? Did he properly identify the assailants? Could he distinguish between the two Egyptians who were working at the club that night?

But Steinberg remained consistent. Cool and unflappable, analytical in every description, and totally believable. He hadn't had much to drink because he never drank much, he said, being a poor medical student and cheap to boot, which his friends corroborated. Without exception, EMT first-responders testified that Steinberg seemed sober and coherent at the scene and had made the correct medical decisions. His sketches of the attack showed even what each defendant had been wearing.

More witnesses for the prosecution, emergency personnel and detectives, repetitive testimony meant to solidify the case, full of details about a young man in crisis, a dead body. The words were chilling. The emergency room doctor talked about cutting off Peter's clothing and how clean-cut he had looked in his button-down business shirt and khaki pants.

The tension was unbearable. I stared at every witness, hung on every word. I was determined to take in every detail. For sustenance, I gazed at the laminated photograph in my hands of the smiling Peter Westra.

We squirmed in our seats, took each other's hands, but we didn't often look at each other. We were spellbound, tightly wound, fragile as glass. Any gesture too obvious might have caused one of us to break into pieces. Mark kept pinching his thumb, my friend Charlie would tell me later.

When there was a recess, we bolted for the courthouse plaza, where, in steamy ninety-five degree August heat, the tension melted. Sometimes then, in a burst of pent-up emotion, we would giggle about the most trivial courtroom image—the bicycle tie, the Coptic cross, a policeman's belly. When the bailiff called us, we shuffled back to our places, switched positions, clutched each other's hands, prepared for more. I remember seeing Lyn hunched down with her elbows on her knees. We were angry at times, exasperated at other times. Often we were weeping.

I felt like the mother and the victim both . . . I felt like I was in Peter's body, stretched out across the pavement . . . I felt like the paramedic arriving on the scene and starting life support. I could have been the juror in the back row, crossing and recrossing her legs and wiping away a tear. Sitting there on that cold hard seat, trying to take it all in, my hand entwined in the hand of the dear man next to me, my heart was also with the father who had lost his only son and with the two stoic young women who had lost their only brother.

I didn't know how I could possibly get up the next day, walk back into the courtroom, and listen to more. But I was compelled to be present for every moment. I reassured myself that we weren't alone, that friends were there to hold us up, and that more friends were supporting us in Minnesota. We'd heard the facts and most of the details earlier, but it was the way in which the facts and details were delivered now that hurt almost more than the information itself. Cold, clinical, detailed recall. Pointed questions, directed questions, impassive responses. Step by step, a case was laid out. A young man died. All of us who listened died with him—again.

THE MEDICAL EXAMINER TOOK THE STAND. I squeezed my eyes shut, trying not to listen, yet trying to grasp the unbearable. "In my opinion, he died of multiple blunt-force injuries to the head and neck," said the county medical examiner who performed the autopsy. He also testified that Peter's blood-alcohol content was 0.209 percent, which was more than twice the legal limit for drivers in New Jersey.

But Peter wasn't driving, I wanted to scream. He and his friends had walked one block from their hotel to the club, and he had intended to walk back from the club to that hotel again. But he didn't make it!

"Isn't it true that someone with a 0.209 BAC would be at greater risk for losing respiration at the time of a loss of consciousness?" asked the defense attorney in an effort to blame the alcohol for Peter's demise.

"No," replied the medical examiner.

Then the defense attorney suggested the brain injury might have occurred in a backward fall onto the pavement.

"There is no evidence of that."

Mercifully, Murray passed the crime scene photos to the jury discreetly so we wouldn't have to see them.

A neuropathologist hired by the prosecution took the stand next. A stiff little old lady who had been schooled in Minnesota, articulate and erudite, she turned to face the jury as she corroborated the testimony of the medical examiner. She had examined Peter's brain after it had been removed during the autopsy. With great authority she said brain hemorrhaging and swelling had caused cardiac arrhythmia, which led to respiratory failure and death. In agony, I listened to her talk of removing Peter's brain, holding it in her hand, cutting it for specimens.

"The trigger for all of this would have been the traumatic injury to the brain," she said.

"Could the injury have occurred from a fall?" asked the defense attorney.

"There's no evidence suggesting he sustained that type of injury from a fall," the neuropathologist said.

Ann put her head in her hands and sobbed. Now a second year medical student, she had just enough experience to understand the medical experts, and for many months after the trial, every time she worked in the emergency room, she told me she'd think of Peter lying on a gurney, dying alone.

The prosecutor called one bouncer who scared the bejesus out of me. Black-haired, black-clothed, he wore a mock turtleneck and a gold chain, looking, one friend said, as though he'd just walked off the set of The Sopranos. Chewing gum and slurring his speech, he was obviously angry to have been subpoenaed by the prosecution, but he'd been working that night in the VIP room, and his testimony was important.

"Were the young men unruly?" Murray asked. "Did they step out of bounds with the dancers?"

"Nah, I dun't see nuthin," he replied. "Nah, they weren't botherin' the girls."

So why did the local newspapers, even during the trial, persist in reporting that Peter had been expelled from the bar for groping the dancers? Groping—a horrible word. It hurt. It was unfair. And it was unsubstantiated. Now even a bar employee refuted it.

O NE AFTERNOON DURING THE SECOND WEEK of the trial, my nephew Mike and his wife said they were going to drive into Atlantic City to look for the club on New York Avenue. I decided to go along, even though I would have preferred to go with Mark to see where Peter had died, but Mark had no interest in seeing the place. I told myself we each were entitled to do as we wished—even in this painful, sordid pilgrimage.

My stomach was tight and my heart heavy as we drove through the streets of the casino town. We turned the corner onto New York Avenue, and there it was—a leftover scrap of a nightclub, bleak and dark. The two-level cinder-block box was so much smaller than I had imagined it being from the floor plan we were shown in court. Not far from the boardwalk, beach and blue sky hovering over and around the tall hotels, the tiny chunk looked more like an old garage on a dirty alley. It sat there solid and solemn, closed months before for a liquor violation.

Around the place where my son had been killed were black-painted concrete blocks, faded and chipped, a marquee of dusty light bulbs, a single window covered with metal grating, a littered empty lot, a dumpster. The door entrance through which Peter had tried to re-enter to get his friend or his credit card or whatever, was an ordinary-sized steel door, like the staff entrance to a factory. I winced as I imagined all the bouncers squeezing through that narrow passage to block my son's body, to throw him back to the pavement . . .

I could scarcely imagine the place at night, neon lights blazing, doormen luring the young men into the club. The pavement was cracked, narrow, and full of weeds. How could Peter's tall frame have even fit in the space between the curb and the door? My God, his head must have nearly touched the wheels of the Honda parked at the curb, the Honda he'd been roughed up on before he tried to reenter the club. Why had he tried to go back into the club? Why hadn't they just locked the putrid little door? Why hadn't they simply called the police?

I could go no further. That ugly place bore not a trace, not a hair, not a molecule of my son. Peter was not in there, so this place would not be with me. I vowed instantly to never talk about it, to try with all my heart and soul to forget it. It was not what I wanted to remember of my son.

LATE IN THE SECOND WEEK, a surprise witness for the prosecution verified Pete Steinberg's testimony. Robert was an off-duty bouncer from northern New Jersey who happened to be hanging out at the downstairs bar of the Naked City at the time of the fracas. He saw a bouncer in a black T-shirt haul Peter down the stairs and take him outside the bar.

"Yeah, I was nosey, being in the entertainment business myself, you know. So I went outside to see what was going on."

He saw the bouncer rough Peter up on the hood of the Honda. After Robert went back to the bar, he saw the bouncer reenter the building and go upstairs.

"I pointed him out to the bartender. I told her to tell her manager that he had a bouncer that was way outa line. He shouldn't be treating patrons that way."

"Do you see that bouncer here in the courtroom?" Murray asked.

"Yeah. He's right there." He pointed to Tamer Shahid.

"Then what happened?" asked Murray.

"A few minutes later, I noticed a few guys hustling toward the front door. I went to the door too and watched what happened."

"What did you see?"

"Excuse my language. They were whupping his ass," he said. "Two of them were giving him body shots. Another was kicking him on the torso. It wasn't a very nice sight."

Again Robert went back into the club, gave his name to the police, and left when they shut it down. He left Atlantic City a few days later and continued with his life. Months later when investigators were preparing the case for the prosecution, they found him in Missouri. Robert immediately said, "Oh, that kid died, didn't he? He died of head injuries, didn't he?"

I could have kissed him. I wrote him a thank you note. Because he himself was a bouncer, he might have refused to rat on another bouncer. Over and over he said in the trial that a bouncer is supposed to get unruly patrons out of the building. The police should have been called, the door locked.

"It was just unreasonable for them to do what they did to this poor guy. You just don't treat patrons the way they treated that kid," he said.

THE DAYS GROUND ON, RELENTLESS and harrowing, one witness after the other, every ounce of my attention focused on the words of attorneys and witnesses. I was desperate to understand what had happened that night.

The defendant remained in his chair, and we could see only half his face. I rarely looked his way. Instead, it was the defense attorney who became the focus of our anger, the one we all loved to hate, for he struck us as ill-prepared, maybe even lazy. He continually lobbed seeds of doubt without building a plausible, cohesive case to counter the prosecution. For a while he pursued a track of mistaken identity, because two of the bouncers were Egyptian.

"Are you sure you saw this bouncer?" he asked, pointing to the six-foot-two, two hundred ten pound bulky Shahid. "Couldn't it have been this barback?" The barback, standing right next to Shahid, was five-foot-six. The two didn't even look the same nationality, much less the same size.

One afternoon the defense attorney pulled five pairs of boots from paper bags and held them high for the jury to see. He implied that the police department's examination of the boots was somehow flawed. He tried to confuse the identification of the boots Steinberg said he saw inflict the kicks to Peter's head. "Don't you think you could have seen *white* tennis shoes with metallic tips at the ends of the laces rather than *black* work boots with metallic toe caps?" He questioned why there wasn't any blood on the boots, even though we had repeatedly been told there wasn't any blood found either at the scene or on Peter's body.

I wanted to scream. His defense strategy was simply to infer carelessness in the prosecution's case, to obfuscate, to confuse. As he hemmed and hawed, grasping at straws and raising incredible scenarios one after another, I looked at him as though he were the devil himself. To me he was malicious. Doing his job, I supposed, but repugnant.

Then we heard he intended to put his client on the stand. Shahid would be the defense's main witness, testifying on his own behalf. What would I think of his version of events? Would I stand up and scream at him? Would I burst out in tears and run out of the courtroom? He would no longer be a shadowy, silent presence sitting next to his attorney, whispering from time to time. He would step forward, walk to the front, open his mouth, tell his story.

And I would stare him in the face.

STEINBERG SAID SHAHID MUST HAVE LOST fifty pounds during the year in jail, but he still looked brutishly big to me. He had a lot to say when he got his chance on the stand, and his attorney let him rip, posing a few simple questions from time to time to keep him going.

As he spoke, he glanced our way, at times looking like a pleading puppy dog, feigning innocence. I stared daggers back at him. He was despicable, delusional, not worthy of an ounce of my pity.

On the stand, Shahid gave the third explanation since his arrest of why he took Peter out of the club. "We were standing next to the bar, just talking. The kid was drunk. He knocked over some beer bottles that were on the bar. The bottles fell on the floor and broke. When the guy bent down to pick up the glass, I got afraid. I didn't know what he was going to do."

So he put Peter in an arm lock, hauled him down the stairs, and roughed him up outside on the hood of the Honda. Then he went back into the club, back upstairs to wash his hands, and, of course, had nothing to do with the subsequent attack that killed Peter.

"No, I wasn't there. I didn't see nothing."

Shahid's explanation sounded well thought out, but ludicrously improbable. Threatened by glass in Peter's hand? So he put him in an armlock? Beat him up but disappeared while Peter was beaten to death by other bouncers? Nobody in the courtroom was persuaded, at least not on our side.

Under cross-examination Murray hammered him. When Shahid rambled, Murray cut into him. "Just answer the question—yes or no?" When he continued to ramble, Murray asked emphatically, "Should I repeat the question one more time?" He made Shahid look like a dufus by asking, "Let's try that again. Did you or didn't you . . . ?"

Once, quite deliberately I think, Murray caused Shahid's anger to flare. When Shahid described the events of July 8 as an accident, Murray jumped all over him.

"What do you mean by 'accident'?" he growled.

Shahid burst out, "Accident! Incident! I don't understand your language!" He hoisted up his shoulders. His eyes narrowed, his lips tightened. In a flash we caught a glimpse of how he might have lost control that night over Peter's body.

At the end of cross-examination, Murray got in front of Shahid, looked him directly in the eyes, and summed up his case.

"He was talking to you, wasn't he? He was in your face, wasn't he? He was sweaty, wasn't he? He put his hand on your shoulder, didn't he? You got mad, didn't you? And so you took him out."

Shahid squirmed and mumbled incoherently. And Murray turned away. The jury stared at Shahid while we silently cheered.

Thirteen

Partial Verdict

Over and over during the three weeks of trial I repeated my mantra: We are not here to hate, not to avenge, not merely to learn what happened on July 8, 2001. We may never know what happened that night, certainly not why. We are here for only one purpose: To love and to honor Peter.

Murray told us on the first day that he never tried to figure out a jury or guess their biases. He saw them as wallpaper, he said, part of the backdrop, and he just went out and presented his case. He said he was too often surprised by a jury in the end to try to anticipate their sympathies before the verdict had been returned.

I too was learning what a crapshoot a jury could be. I had been raised to believe in a system of a justice determined by one's peers, but that belief had never been tested. In this group of twelve jurors and two alternates, there were no fundraisers or attorneys, no Minnesotans, no one who was visiting Atlantic City for the first time, and no one who abhorred being there. This group of jurors did not feel like my peers.

The jurors never uttered a word as they filed in and out of the jury box several times each day, water bottles in hand, sweaters over their shoulders, the women toting big satchels. Sometimes we'd cross their paths at the courthouse door or in the parking lot as they got in their cars to drive home. They probably resented this intrusion into their daily lives too. Among the seven women and five men, ten who were white and two who were black, there was one woman in her late twenties, who would prove pivotal, one man in his seventies, and several like us in their mid-fifties—parents, I imagined, who tried to keep their children out of harm's way, parents of sons who partied. I presumed a few would be concerned about despicable acts of violence happening in their county, about seedy bars and the brutal behavior of bar employees, about how such frequent acts of violence might hamper lucrative tourism.

The charge to the jury was complicated, in three parts: aggravated assault (for the beating itself), conspiracy to commit aggravated assault (all five of the men joining up to do the beating), and murder. On the murder charge, the jury could find Shahid innocent but guilty of reckless manslaughter—the third degree; guilty of aggravated manslaughter—the second degree; or guilty of murder—the first degree. To be guilty of murder, the jury would have to decide that Shahid purposely or knowingly caused Peter's death. It was not necessary to prove his motive.

Early on, Murray told us a verdict of murder in New Jersey would be highly unlikely without a murder weapon. "What about those big black boots the defendant was wearing?" I asked him. "Weren't those weapons?"

"Articles of clothing worn as clothing, as opposed to being wielded as weapons—such as a belt used in a strangling—are not considered weapons of murder," he calmly replied.

So a verdict of aggravated manslaughter was the most we could hope for.

In New Jersey aggravated manslaughter meant the defendant engaged in reckless and conscious behavior that he knew would *probably* cause the death of the victim. The lesser verdict of reckless manslaughter meant the jury deemed that the defendant engaged in reckless and conscious behavior that he knew would *possibly* cause the death of the victim. A verdict of aggravated manslaughter would put Shahid away for ten to thirty years. A verdict of reckless manslaughter would put him away for five to ten years.

The jury's deliberations seemed endless. Hours blended into days. We never wandered far from the courthouse for fear the jury would return with a verdict that would be read by the judge whether we were there or not. So we hung around the corridors, tried to play cards, tried to avoid the defendant's family, or stood on the plaza outside in the sun. Small talk was awkward. We were all lost in our own thoughts, feelings, and silent prayers.

When the jury returned a couple of times for further explanation of the charges, we would rush back in. Every time the jury entered or exited the courtroom, we were in our places in the front row. I wondered what they were thinking? Which ones were the fathers? The mothers?

We waited . . . and paced. I shivered with cold even though it was ninety degrees outside. Every inch of my body was taut, screaming for justice. Sitting by myself, I began to pray for the jurors' wisdom, for their will to do the right thing.

Adrenaline shot through me every time we were called back into the courtroom—maybe there would be a verdict. But no, over and over the jury had more questions. When they wanted to review the videotaped testimony of Steinberg, Robert, and the neuropathologist—an entire day's worth of testimony that would take hours to replay—the judge decided there wasn't enough time left that afternoon. Because he never held court on Fridays, he called a recess until the following Monday. More waiting.

Three or four reporters had been hanging around, waiting for a statement. Mark told them we felt disappointed. Ann started to whimper, and soon we were all weeping. Tension eased, but despair crept in. Mark hung his head as we clung to each other. "I just want to get on with my life," he said.

On Monday we watched the six hours of video replay. Hard enough to experience the first time, I was relieved the video monitor was turned slightly toward the jury so I couldn't totally see the images. Instead I studied the jurors: so little expression on their faces, so little giveaway about their sentiments or inclinations. But I wondered how they could help but be moved?

When the playback finished, the jury resumed deliberations. I prayed for God to help them do the right thing—for Peter's sake. We needed justice for Peter. . . . Someone other than us needed to pay a price. I sought revenge, I knew, from a court of justice.

The jury returned again at the end of the afternoon, and the foreman reported they were deadlocked ten to two. The judge, visibly annoyed, grumbled about their needing to take their work more seriously. He wanted a verdict. He begrudgingly called a recess and ordered the jury to return the next morning.

I had no idea if I was angry or sad or more angry than sad or more sad than angry. I feared not being able to name my feelings or focus them. I was horribly afraid of feeling disillusioned, abandoned, misunderstood, discredited. I was afraid my system of justice would fail me.

Later, much later, I would realize that my view then of the system was flawed. I thought it was Peter who was on trial—his behavior that night, the behavior of his friends, our parenting. But the jury didn't care about us. It was Shahid they were considering. To them we were merely spectators and whether or not our presence made any difference in the end, we would never know.

Murray warned us about a mistrial, but he too thought the jury hadn't yet worked hard enough to come to agreement. "Way too soon to scream mistrial," he said.

After another morning without a verdict, Murray exhorted the increasingly impatient judge to make the jury deliberate longer. "It's too soon to let them quit," Murray implored. "They've deliberated fewer than three hours in one sitting."

We waited another afternoon. Counting the weekend, we had now been waiting five days. I was at my lowest point. A former pastor of ours who was living in New Jersey had been waiting at the courthouse with us. On a break during proceedings he gave me his Bible and a piece of paper listing some verses. I started to pray.

I felt as though I were at the foot of the cross. I felt the silence and the agony of Jesus waiting to die. At his lowest point, just before he died, Jesus prayed for compassion: *Forgive them, Lord, for they know not what they do.*

I prayed nonstop simply for a decision. Help the jurors do the right thing, Lord. Please let them just decide. Help them to settle their struggles, their conflicts, and their disagreements. Help them listen to one another. Help them examine their own points of view, be willing to change, be willing to compromise. Please, Lord, help them decide.

Earlier on, Murray had said, "You just never know." The two black jurors could have been offended by a young police officer's racial slur early in the trial or two jurors simply might not like private college students, or people from Minnesota, or well-dressed young men in blue shirts and blue jackets.

Murray was as helpless as anyone to console us. "I just don't know what to tell you people," he said. "It's a rotten system, but it's better than any other."

AFTER THREE DAYS, THE JURY DECIDED they couldn't decide. They were deadlocked. Hung. They could not agree on the murder component of the charge, the jury did convict Shahid of aggravated assault and conspiracy to commit aggravated assault. He'd do time even without the murder verdict. The judge called a mistrial.

To avoid double jeopardy—trying Shahid twice for the same crime—the judge accepted, but did not officially enter the verdicts. Shahid would remain in jail but would not be officially sentenced until after he was tried again for murder. Murray assured us he would retry Shahid for murder, but he said it would not happen for months. Meanwhile, the four others who participated in the beating remained free on bail, awaiting their own trial on charges of aggravated assault.

We were aghast. We could barely understand: partially, but not totally convicted? Double jeopardy—like in the movies? It was an outcome we had never expected.

We wept and hugged each other as we crawled from the courtroom to face reporters who had been waiting for days for statements. Though we hadn't discussed what we'd say, Mark stepped forward and spoke for us all in words that sounded almost rehearsed. "This has been a tremendous ordeal for our family. We're disappointed it's not over." He said he thought the evidence was overwhelming. He praised the prosecutor.

Then he left the reporters with thoughts of Peter. "Listening to Shahid, nothing he said had anything to do with Peter. Peter wasn't the type to get into fights, provoke people, or act irresponsibly. He was a friendly, garrulous young man who always wanted people to like him. . . No sentence that's given to Tamer Shahid will change what happened to Peter or lessen our pain. We're not here to get revenge or to inflict pain on Tamer to assuage our own. We're here to love and honor Peter."

We were all disappointed. Within a couple hours we bid tearful good-byes to our daughters—Ann back to medical school in Baltimore and Lyn off for her senior year of college in Maine. Mark and I caught the next flight to Minneapolis.

It would have been easy to direct our frustration and anger toward the judicial system, toward this jury that just couldn't reach agreement. But I hesitated. I hadn't been with them, and I didn't know their issues. So I decided to hold tight to Murray's assessment: a rotten system, but better than any other.

I clung to our purpose for being there, stated by Mark and echoed the next day in the newspapers. "We didn't come for revenge, but to love and honor Peter."

The day after we got home, Jackie called to say a juror wanted to talk to us. Though she reminded us we didn't need to talk to the juror, we decided to return the phone call in the hope of learning what had happened during jury deliberations. We got an earful.

The juror we talked to told us one particular juror, the woman we remembered as the youngest and prettiest, the one who could have dated any of the young men who had testified for the prosecution, had refused to find Shahid guilty of causing Peter's death. She had agreed Shahid was present with the others at the beating—and she therefore found him guilty of assault—but she would not find him guilty of murder.

We learned she was a current employee of the Tun Tavern, where the bachelor party had gathered for dinner before going to the Naked City. We wondered if that should have disqualified her as a juror in the beginning, but Murray insisted where people worked at the time of the trial rather than at the time of the crime, wasn't relevant. In Atlantic County, a lot of potential jurors worked in casino-related businesses, he said.

The juror on the phone said the young woman had been adamant that the testimony of Peter's friends and the off-duty bouncer was prejudiced and could not be believed. She seemed so unbending that the other jurors thought she might have been approached during the trial; they even tried at one point to get her removed from the jury before voting. The juror on the phone was apologetic. Several jurors, she said, felt awful about the verdict, and would be living with the case for a long time.

Though knowing what had happened during deliberations helped, we certainly didn't feel any better about the outcome.

I retreated into myself. I didn't want to see anyone. I didn't want pity, though I did feel pitiable. I didn't want to be urged to be strong, to be brave, to try to get past it, to get on. I could hear the voices, and I had plenty of my own.

Withdrawn as I was, I still didn't want to be avoided. I wanted the questions. I wanted to be understood. I wanted everybody to understand that this travail would always be part of us, part of our lives that we would never forget. We would be bereaved parents, first and foremost, for the rest of our lives.

In a desperate effort to communicate to those who cared, I sent an e-mail a few days after returning home from the trial.

Of all the possible outcomes, I never imagined a mistrial. I hardly know what to say about it. I barely understand and certainly feel incapable of explaining to others all the legal technicalities, jeopardy issues, and retrial ramifications. So I, the queen of the parlance of grief, am tongue-tied while Mark, more reticent to wear his equally hurting heart on his sleeve, can talk about the trial quite intelligently and even dispassionately. But, in short, I feel quite let down.

...Casinos, beaches, go-carts, miniature golf and strip clubs—much to lure thirteen adventurous, ambitious, successful, maybe slightly naïve young men who just wanted to be together to celebrate the wedding of their friend. My discomfort with the locals only grew as the trial progressed. One juror was dismissed because she realized she knew the brother of a bouncer who was a witness. Another was dismissed when she realized she lived in the same neighborhood as another bouncer-witness and she grew afraid. To me, it's entirely conceivable that the intransigent juror (who turned out to be working now at the same restaurant where the thirteen had dined that night!) could have been tainted. Something is very wrong indeed when after the verdict is read the defense attorney asks for a police escort to his car.

We find no fault whatsoever in Murray's prosecution. Jackie and others from his staff comforted us constantly. The tone was set in their opening arguments and then supported through the cogent, bright-eyed testimony of the groom, the best man, the friend left behind in the bar who knew nothing, and, most significantly, brave, brilliant Pete Steinberg and all the police investigators who interviewed him. The thirteen boys simply had no idea what a cesspool they had walked into. Bad decisions, disastrous consequences. In no way did Peter Westra deserve to die. Not one witness who didn't work at the bar said they saw Peter harassing the dancers. But it doesn't matter. We now know without a doubt that Peter Westra was just being Peter—drunk, yes, friendly, but trying to engage the defendant in conversation, putting his hand ("his sweaty hand," as Murray said) on the bouncer's shoulder, who went ballistic.

I don't mean to sound spiteful or completely disillusioned, but I realize now that whatever justice is gained, for Peter's sake, will be too little, too late. Of course we knew no good outcome was possible. Peter wasn't going to come home with us.

We went to New Jersey with one purpose firmly front of mind: to love and to honor Peter. And we did a damn good job of it. And we're still a family.

And we're luckier than many families that have lost loved ones. We know what happened to Peter. We got his body back and spread his ashes on the lake near our home. And we know, thanks to God, that he didn't suffer. Peter is a fabulous son. He is—and forever will be—home with us.

*   With love, Mary*

Part Two
After the Trial

Tonight all the hells of young grief have opened up again; the mad words, the bitter resentment, the fluttering in the stomach, the nightmare reality, the wallowed-in tears. For in grief nothing "stays put." One keeps on emerging from a phase, but it always recurs. Round and round. Everything repeats. Am I going in circles, or dare I hope I am on a spiral?

—C.S. Lewis, from *Healing After Loss* by Martha Whitmore Hickman

Peter, age seventeen, after winning the state soccer tournament.

Fourteen

Time

W ill you be all right?" Mark asked as we unpacked our trial clothes and tucked our suitcases under Peter's bed.

"Uh-huh," I mumbled with a sigh.

He gave me a tentative hug, and then he left to check in at his office. I was alone and miserable. I looked around Peter's room—the big new bed purchased just before he died in which he had never slept, the photos on top of his chest of drawers, the terry-cloth robe on a hook in his closet—and I fell to the floor. I beat my fists on the carpet and cried my heart out as I hadn't since the day we got the news of his death.

I went down to the dock and sat on the bench, hugging myself. I felt cold, though it was a warm late-August afternoon, and I wanted that warmth to coat me. The lake looked vast, wide open, barren. It seemed inscrutable, unchanging, unforgiving. I noticed no birds, no ducks, no boaters. I had no thoughts, no specific feelings. My body felt heavy as lead.

The next morning I had coffee with good friends who had kept in touch with me during the trial. I knew they cared about me and Mark, but by their questions I sensed they hadn't paid complete attention to what we had gone through in New Jersey. They hadn't hung on our every e-mailed word. I was a bit surprised . . . and disappointed. They weren't as caught up in the trial as we were. Their lives had gone on.

I was humbled. So tightly bound in my cocoon of grief over the past year, I hadn't realized everybody's life didn't stop with the death of Peter.

We would get a new trial but we had no idea when. It could be months before the process got going again. None of our friends seemed to understand we would be waiting on tenterhooks until the judicial process was completed. The details of the process were too obscure for most of them anyway, and, with unfolding so far away under the jurisdiction of another state with its own rules and customs, people just didn't know what questions to ask. My closest friends were trying, trying very hard, but none could walk in my shoes.

Meanwhile, Mark and I tried to resume the pace of our lives. Mark worked long days in the same all-consuming legal position he'd had for a couple decades with the same few clients who had by now become good friends. I started my new position as development director for a non-profit publishing company. Though I wasn't as busy as Mark, I was grateful to be out of the house, away from the shell of my former life.

But I hated getting home before him. I'd run errands, visit my mother, or sit at my desk, anything to avoid that hulking specter of our used-to-be-perfect life. Our home yelled to me of had beens, what ifs, could have beens. In the shortening autumn days, Mark and I created coping rituals: I'd leave all the lights on when I left the house in the morning, and he'd turn them all off before he shut the side door to go. Home was not the comfortable refuge it used to be.

Weekends dragged. We had no energy for projects or entertaining or even cooking well for ourselves. I'd wear Peter's sweaters, hoping to feel closer to him, or more inspired, but instead I felt lazy. Time was heavy. We slept late, putzed, walked, biked, or, often, worked. We tried going to movies, but there were few we could tolerate because of their violence or reminders of Peter.

Soon after I'd started, I began to grow uneasy about my new job, which threw me further off-kilter. Maybe I'd made a mistake. I felt confused about my fundraising role in the small organization and sensed an uncomfortable distance among my colleagues. I didn't feel welcome, and I wasn't sure I'd ever feel successful. I questioned whether or not to continue trying, but decided to persevere because I believed I had something to offer, and because I didn't want to fail. Furthermore, I didn't have the energy to pursue anything else.

Then suddenly we had a new trial date, November 4, fewer than two months off. We had new hope the judicial process might be concluded by Thanksgiving. Mark called the imminent trial date a mixed blessing, for he had hoped to let it fade into the background a bit, to be able to get on with his life. I called it a good sign that bode well for the case. Somebody, I thought, wanted to move the process along, get it done. I was hopeful.

Everyone asked if we would go again to another trial. Of course we had to see it through. Now I felt prepared. I knew how tense, demanding, and cruel another trial would be. Privately, I couldn't help but wonder how it would change me further, change my family, harden all of us. How would we be in the end? Already, a little more than a month after the mistrial, I sensed the judicial process had changed me as much as Peter's death had.

Then, just as suddenly, the retrial was postponed. The defense attorney got himself removed from the case because he hadn't been paid by the defendant. During the trial we had resented that defense attorney, but we appreciated his ineptitude was probably helpful to our case. Changing attorneys at this point would mean a huge delay in going to trial again. Pete Steinberg and Mark each wrote short passionate letters to the judge, urging him not to let the attorney off, exhorting a speedy conclusion. Nevertheless, the judge decided to let him off the case.

We were bitterly disappointed . . . again. I had little sympathy for a private attorney who didn't make certain he'd be paid in adequate installments during the process of a trial. Now the defendant was free to seek another one, which could take months. How would he pay a second private attorney anyway? When would this end?

I wanted to cry, but Charlie told me to get angry. "Get real, Mary. Get mad." What good would it do to get mad?

Instead I felt my faith falter—my faith in human nature, my faith in the judicial system. Hope—for closure, for resolution, for peace—waned. Yet I was supposed to go on day by day, doing my best, taking the lumps, maintaining my dignity and my grace. It was too much. Unfair. Unrealistic. It was simply too much shit to shoulder.

IN THE FREEZING DRIZZLE OF MID-OCTOBER, with no interest in one last quick ride around the lake for Peter, Mark and I hauled the boat out of the water for winter. We put Peter's slalom ski in the garage attic next to his snow skis, his hockey sticks, his skateboard in its blue and white fake-leather carrying case. We put away our patio furniture—all five chairs.

Sitting on my bench at the dock, enveloped in my rain parka, I watched the birds head south. I wondered whether they knew where they were going? What they'd see? What would become of them? They'll go beyond the horizon, I said to myself. Yes, that horizon . . . the world beyond, that we cannot see . . . the world I await, in which I'll see Peter again and God and all the rest.

I waited for the other shoe to drop . . . for more gloom, for doom. I felt more fatalistic than ever before. What difference could I possibly make in the outcome of the judicial process? Why should I expend the effort, the hope? Why keep my faith?

Everything felt beyond my control. One night, after making love, Mark still lying on top of me, I stroked the contour of his shoulder blades with my fingers. He was the only one in the world to know what it felt like to lose his son, Peter. I started to cry with the sad realization that not even Mark would be with me forever.

Everything seemed to be about time these days. We heard it over and over again in court: thirty years for murder, ten to thirty years for aggravated manslaughter, five to ten years for reckless manslaughter. Shahid had already been in jail for a year. We'd been waiting for justice for more than a year.

But what about Peter's time? How much time did the bouncers give him?

He had lived for 8,922 days, but there were so many more days left in that healthy young body. I had lived for 21,045 days, and I wasn't even old. Yet now we had an eternity ahead of us . . . all the rest of our days without our son. But how much time did we have as a couple?

I heard the voice of Peter coming to me again: Take care of Dad, Mom. Take care of Dad.

Yes, Peter, you're so right. I will try. Thank you, Peter.

MARK GOT HIS TIME WITH PETER when I was out of town for the funeral of Charlie's mother. Since Peter's death, we had rarely spent a night apart. In my absence, he stayed up late watching television, surfing the channels for something to capture his attention. He landed on the Tom Green Show, a program we'd heard about but never seen, popular with the twenty-something crowd, one of Peter's favorites. We knew that in

Manhattan Peter and Mac had played on a roller hockey team with some of the crew from the show. We thought they must have gone to one of the shows, because Mac had given us a photo of the guys with Tom Green. So Mark decided to see what it was all about.

As Mark was watching the show, Green said something funny and the camera panned the audience. The camera panned the audience, and landed on Peter. Yes. Peter was on TV—the full screen—laughing, enjoying himself. Unmistakably Peter!

Mark was dumbfounded. The next morning he called Mac, who confirmed they had indeed been to a show, eighteen months before. Mac said he would try to get us a copy of the tape at his next roller hockey practice with the crew. A couple weeks later, the tape came in the mail, and I too got to see Peter on TV! But Mark saw him first, home alone, late one night, when he normally would have been asleep. Mark usually pooh-poohed miracles, but he soon acknowledged that it was truly a gift from a son to his father.

On November 8, 2002, sixteen months after the day of Peter's death, I left twenty bucks in his honor for the employees at the coffee shop I frequented, because they'd been kind to me and because my son always told me to be more patient and kind with sales people. I took time that day to look through Peter's photo albums, found photos of him when he was sixteen years old, because he'd been dead sixteen months. I wondered what I'd do at twenty-five months, when there wouldn't be any more photos.

On his sixteenth birthday, he looked so young, gawky, somehow still unformed, in braces and barely taller than Ann. He looked eager and strong in his soccer jersey, number 8, and in his cross-country ski clothes. I saw him dressed up, polished and spiffed, for the Valentine's dance, posed next to Ann, a sophisticated senior. A month later we were in on vacation, where he scampered on rocks, toted a big camera bag on his shoulder, sandaled and T-shirted.

He looked more grown up by his seventeenth birthday. Proudly posed in a tux for a formal dance, he had stretched out, lost his gawkiness, gained confidence in debate and varsity soccer, and was the oldest kid at home since Ann went off for college. The responsible big brother, Peter drove his younger sister, Lyn, to school every day, let her sit shotgun in the front seat even though he picked up other kids. She worshipped him.

THOUGH USUALLY MOTIVATED TO BETTER behavior by memories of my son, I did something I knew he wouldn't likely approve of. I bugged his friend, Pete Steinberg, and wrote my heart out to him. A sermon based on Luke 10: 25-37, the parable of the Good Samaritan, about the power of human kindness and the injunction to "go and do likewise" to help one's neighbor, had inspired me. The images of a man traveling from Jerusalem to Jericho, besieged by robbers who strip him of all his clothing, wound him, and leave him half-dead, struck all too close to home. I saw my son on the pavement in front of the sleazy club, knocked to the ground, kicked repeatedly in the head and torso, and left for dead, in fact already nearly dead, by everyone except his friend, Pete. I saw my son abandoned, as the man in the parable had been, and his friend, the only one present, making the effort to help him, to save him, to "bandage his wounds." I saw Pete Steinberg pouring on oil and wine and holding his head. The images took my breath away. I felt so terribly sad and sorry about the final moments of Peter's life.

So I got up in the middle of the night, went downstairs to the round table in the family room, and wrote a hurried note to Steinberg. I thanked him for trying so desperately and courageously to save my son's life, for being there with him in his final moments, for helping us keep his spirit alive.

Then I thanked God for Pete, for other dear friends, and for all the Good Samaritans who had come when they heard of Peter's death and who continued to come simply because they loved every one of us and knew it was the right thing to do. It took so little—watermelon soap left in the mailbox, popcorn mailed to the girls, a phone message devoid of pity, a book or a poem—to show compassion and love. Gestures like the Good Samaritan's. I am grateful.

AT THANKSGIVING WE MET THE GIRLS in Washington DC because it was a short hop for Ann from Baltimore and an easy flight for Lyn from college in Maine. Knocking around museums, going to good restaurants, walking and talking, we tried hard to get used to being a family of four—mom and dad and two grown daughters. I was a bit taken aback by how easily we flowed as a foursome. We fit more conveniently now around a table in a restaurant and even strolling city sidewalks was simpler. We moved along in a tight line, often arm in arm, sometimes in couples holding hands. Each girl had a parent at her wing, close by, accessible, unhampered by a pesky, talkative brother.

One afternoon while walking between museums on the mall, I suddenly noticed my charm bracelet was missing from my wrist. It wasn't an expensive bracelet, but it had been given to me recently by a friend who remembered Peter with specific charms—a French flag, a soccer ball, hearts, and stars. I spent a couple hours retracing my steps, talking to guards in museums, annoyed with myself and desperate to find it. I knew I could replace it, but I knew I wouldn't, because *that* was the bracelet I wanted. Finally, Ann said, "Where would you rather lose it than on a holiday with your daughters?" and she was right. Perhaps the bracelet had served its purpose. I stopped my frantic search. My daughters were more important than any piece of jewelry.

Months later, when Lyn was home from spring break and went to my closet to borrow a sweater, she rediscovered that charm bracelet—stuck to the long-sleeved shirt I had worn that day in Washington. It had slipped off my wrist when I pulled off the shirt, yet it stayed attached to the fabric. I put it back on my wrist, another little mystery. Sometimes I felt totally taken care of in ways I couldn't understand but wholeheartedly accepted.

W E STUMBLED THROUGH THE HOLIDAY SEASON. We went to a few social gatherings but we were anything but the life of the parties. I still didn't drink and I didn't smile very often either. I hung around the fringes and found someone I really wanted to talk with—usually a young mother, for I preferred hearing about busy little kids and the making of traditions. Talk about college and older kids coming home for the holidays, about families reuniting, sent me into another room.

I was tempted to sit my young-mom friends down, or write them letters, urging them to slow down, to savor the seasons, to grab the memories. How I used to run myself ragged—coping with the kids' schedules, staying up late at night to accomplish what I thought was really important, and feeling angry when Mark was distracted with his typically heavy year-end business. I wanted to tell my young-mom friends not to take Christmas so seriously or so personally. What the children would remember wasn't the perfect meal or gift or tree, but the traditions that become family folklore. Young mothers, I wanted to scream, bake cookies *with* the kids, *help* them wrap the gifts, *sit* with them on the couch.

I didn't write the moms. Maybe they already understood that their days with their children were numbered. They didn't need lessons from me.

I always believed there would be a reward for my efforts at home-making. I expected to have a rosy family life forever. I expected our traditions to endure, happy moods to prevail, love to be secure and everlasting. I counted on the future.

Yet I wasn't totally inflexible about our traditions. After all, I gave up the Rondeau family tradition—serving rabbit for Christmas Eve dinner—when I finally noticed my grown kids pushing it around their plates. Traditions are not forever. Neither joy nor security is guaranteed. I had become part of a not-insignificant segment of the population who found the holidays painful. Now I wanted to skip them, to hide, to flee. I just couldn't find the joy.

I FELT ESPECIALLY CLOSE TO PETER on December 8, a Sunday, when, digging deeper through the Christmas boxes from our attic than I had the year before, I came across one box labeled "Peter's Tree Stuff." I doubt it had been opened since his college years. In the box, I found a two-foot tall artificial tree with two strings of lights, red beads, and a coil of tacky aluminum stars twisted tightly to the stem, right up to the tip. It was just as he had last decorated it. A few ski ornaments still clung to the tree's plastic needles. In the bottom of the box, I found other ornaments, snowmen on skis, more of those that I had sent to him during college. I cursed him as I uncoiled the tightly wrought string of lights that no longer worked. But I hated to tamper with his creativity, however haphazard. I remembered the cutout cardboard earrings he had painted for me on a Christmas morning when he was about twelve. Very clever, but quite ugly. I had a hard time wearing them. A year ago, I tried to wear them just for fun, but the gesture felt belated.

Mark and I lit that little tree and didn't turn the lights off for a month. We have continued to light it every year, one of the first Christmas decorations with which I bother. We set it in his room on the cedar trunk that holds many of his possessions. The trunk was a suggestion of other bereaved parents who couldn't decide what to do with their son's belongings. Bright lights, ski ornaments, and aluminum stars shone night and day and greeted us with warmth as we passed through his room to get to our computer. That little tree shouted out love.

Our second holiday season without Peter went better than the first one. The difference was a subtle, more settled feeling. If we couldn't be downright happy, we were trying harder to be content. Mark, the girls, and I more fully enjoyed each other's company, worked harder to please one another, to be more of a family. Feeling the sadness of Peter's absence less acutely, we were more able to vividly sense his presence.

I brought up Peter's name, gently and casually. We talked about him, or often just included his name while we talked about what we used to do as a family. The girls rarely discussed their grief, the trial, or how they had managed to cope. Their grief felt like an untouchable subject, one I thought I shouldn't push.

It was I who was probably most sensitive to the hole in our family, and sometimes I felt let down, for I wanted Peter to be our third, albeit missing, child, still their brother, still an important member of our family. I wanted to talk about him and to hear the girls talk about him. Always I wanted . . . I wished . . . though I was gradually but slowly realizing I didn't always rule in this new family of four adults. I couldn't always get what I wanted.

When it was time for Lyn to return to college in January, I wasn't ready to say good-bye. For me, her visit had been too short and too busy with too many friends, too much cookie baking, gift wrapping, and, of course, sleeping. I had not had enough sitting and chatting, and I had no idea how she was really doing. To me, she seemed distracted and anxious. I felt helpless to truly help her.

As I was dropping her off at the airport and helping her carry her bags from the car to the baggage check, a young man on the curbside caught my attention. I said to Lyn, "Doesn't he look a bit like Peter?"

"No, Mom, he doesn't look like Peter at all." A minute later she said, "Is that all you think about?"

When I protested and said no, of course not, she retorted, "It sure seems like over the last two weeks that's all you thought about."

I was stunned, but I didn't say anything. Later, when I was home again and Lyn was on the plane, I processed what I could have said: "No, Lyn, he's not all I think about, but I sure do think about him nearly constantly. I think about you, too, nearly constantly. But I think about you with question marks: What's up? What are you doing? Are you happy? What are you think-ing, hoping, planning? My questions for you are all forward leaning: What kind of person will you become? However, with Peter, my questions are all backward leaning, because he's dead and his future is over. The only question now is, What could he have become? And why? Unlike you, Lyn, he lives only when I think about him, when I remember what he looked like, what he used to do, how he used to act. Otherwise, it's a zero. And for me the zero is unbearable. To not talk about Peter is to forget Peter, to pretend he didn't matter. I can't do that. To talk about him out loud is to verify his existence, to authenticate his birth, his death, our loss.

"If you'd talk about Peter, Lyn, maybe I wouldn't have to so much. Then I'd know that you love him still, that you haven't forgotten him. It would reassure me and comfort me, and I think it might comfort you too. At least it would acknowledge the common bond between us and Peter: mother and son, mother and daughter, brother and sister. I wish you'd talk about him without my bringing him up. I wish . . . but my wishing is selfish. You will be what you will be."

But I didn't say any of that to her. Later, talking with my therapist, I realized how wrong I was to have brought up a Peter-look-alike as Lyn was trying to tackle the business of getting on a plane. It was poor timing on my part. I would apologize to Lyn and vow to be more sensitive, but I feared I would err many more times in this business of parenting my remaining children while grieving a lost one. Finding the balance was difficult.

It took me a long time to learn that Lyn indeed talked plenty about her brother, in her own way, to her own friends. She has often ex-tended her own hand to others who have lost siblings. My dear daughter.

Late one cold January evening, I strode down the hill to the icy lake to discard the remaining greens and five faded red roses of our Christmas table bouquet. I was stern with myself and tried to talk myself into being more hopeful. I made a few promises to the angels of the frozen lake who were watching over Peter's ashes. Sitting on the snowy steps, I threw a wilted rose out for each member of my family and told myself to make some good, somehow, come from this loss. Somehow I had to get myself resigned to the death of my son, accept it, and move on. Then, just as I was chiding myself, a shooting star streamed across the sky. I smiled . . . Peter was wink-ing at me. He was endorsing my hope, telling me again in a mysterious way I could barely understand, "You can do it, Mom."

Fifteen

Winter

I n late January 2003, a year and a half after Peter's murder, Murray
called to tell us the second trial would again be delayed because
Shahid had hired a new private defense attorney, and the new attorney
would need time to prepare his own case. We couldn't grasp how Shahid,
still in jail, or his family had resources to pay a second private attorney
when they hadn't been able to pay the first.

"Who in the world would take his case under such circumstances?" I asked Murray. But Murray didn't know, or didn't tell us.

"Whatever!" was all we could say. We would probably end up
spending the following August again in New Jersey. At least we'd know
what weather to expect. Small consolation. We'd retained our confidence
in Murray, the prosecutor. Another consolation. Most important, Shahid
remained in jail, convicted for the assault on our son. But the consolations
did not build contentment.

The other four perpetrators—two bouncers, the owner, and the
manager of the club where Peter was murdered—were free on bail, going
about their business. I feared the elapse of time might mean witnesses
would not be able to recall the details of our specific case. There was so
much crime in that city.

A TLANTIC CITY, TAGGED BY THE MAGAZINE, *MONEY*, in the late eighties
as the worst place to live in all of America, had in its heyday been one of
the country's most popular middle-class resorts. It was supposedly the

Peter at age thirteen.

home of saltwater taffy, its streets the inspiration for the American version of Monopoly. I remember the allure of the nearly six-mile boardwalk from watching the Miss America pageant on television with my grade-school girlfriends each fall. The city had fallen on hard times since those halcyon days. The beach lost its allure, and the approval of casino gambling in 1976 changed the focus for tourism. When Trump opened the forty-two-story, twelve hundred-room Taj Mahal in 1990, with four football fields of gaming space and three thousand slot machines, the average tourist was spending six hours there, coming by car and moving along the concrete corridors, unaware of the drug-infested tenements and desolate streets just behind the hotels.

Bryant Simon, in his 2004 book *Boardwalk of Dreams: Atlantic City and the Fate of Urban America*, chronicles the decline. "Despite providing 43,924 jobs (almost 15,000 more jobs than Atlantic City's total population), $6 billion in investment (more than the total investment in New Jersey's four other major cities combined over the last quarter century), and even more in taxes (the casinos have paid $5.5 billion to the state and currently contribute 80 percent of the city's total property taxes), the gaming industry has not saved Atlantic City." Today thirty-five million people visit the boardwalk and casinos each year, though, according to FBI data, crime in the city is about three times the U.S. average, and the murder rate is twice the national average. Reporting on the opening of the city's fifteenth casino-megahotel, the Borgata, in 2003, Dan Ackman of *Forbes* wrote, "Atlantic City remains dangerous and depraved."

I was a victim of this seedy city and its out-of-control thugs. Peter had become one of its statistics. Often I felt as if I were wearing an M for murder on my breast, such a social stigma, an object lesson about what can go wrong in a good family from a good community when a boy strays too far from home, away from the safety net of his family's values, to an ugly place where he doesn't pay attention to the dangers lurking around him.

Homicide was the second leading cause of death in the country for young people. Of people between the ages fifteen to twenty-four who died, 21.3 percent died by homicide.

Homicide takes its toll on survivors. One study reported that after five years, sixty-six percent of parents of homicide victims still found no meaning in life. They no longer trusted society or what others might do.

Even after five years, according to this study, 27.7 percent of mothers and 12.5 percent of fathers met criteria for post-traumatic stress disorder.

We were determined to break those odds. We did not want to be victims. And we intentionally tried not to live as victims.

DURING THE LONG MINNESOTA WINTER, Mark and I slowly re-established a comfortable routine, one with its own momentum, something more than mere survival. We bought a treadmill and an exercise bike and worked out together in the mornings. Sometimes we drove together to work. In the evenings, we ate dinner together, and then watched television or read together on the couch.

We went a couple nights a week to our local health club for spinning, an aerobics routine on stationary bikes with an instructor shouting out cadences while we sweaty athletes pedal to music. One evening, I went alone because Mark was working late. I was pedaling hard to REM, a favorite of Peter's. I remembered giving him their CD *Automatic for the People* when he was in high school, and then closing the door to his room so I wouldn't have to hear the raucous music. Now I couldn't get enough of "Everybody Hurts." I teared up at the refrain: "Everybody cries, and everybody hurts sometimes." And when I heard, "hold on, hold on, hold on," I wanted to scream, "I'm trying!"

In the locker room after my workout, a young mom getting dressed near me was bragging about her teenagers and complaining about how they always wanted to do stuff with her when she wanted time alone. Though I tried to refrain, I was soon spouting off that she should encourage them while she could, before they grew up, before they left her household. She agreed, and then she proceeded to tell me about her kids while getting dressed. Eventually she inquired about mine. I hesitated . . . I told her about the girls . . . then I paused. Finally, I pulled Peter's picture from my purse.

Only when she said she thought she recognized him and asked his name did I blurt out the ugly facts about his death, slam-bam, thank-you-ma'am-style, no softened or smoothed detail. After all, she had asked. Then I grabbed my stuff and bolted for the door.

"But at least I'm here and I'm exercising!" I shouted over my shoulder.

She and another woman yelled after me, "Way to go!"

W E SPENT PETER'S WOULD-BE twenty-sixth birthday, the second one since his death, in Santa Fe at the home of our friends Bob and Be. We couldn't ignore the day and we didn't want to go to work. It felt good to get away. The girls couldn't be with us, yet we felt the by-now-familiar ambivalence: we don't want to depend on our friends, but we don't want to be alone.

In Santa Fe, Mark and I took an early morning hike alone up Anatalya. We wore our Middlebury hike T-shirts with Peter's name on the back, and climbed with spunk over snowfields as though Peter's hand were on our backs. In the afternoon, wearing my "Peter Inspires Me" T-shirt, we hiked with Bob and Be at Tent Rocks, feeling energetic to be outside, together, healthy and active. Over and over I mumbled to myself, "Thank you, Lord, for the life of Peter, who inspires us still."

Talking to the girls over the phone in the evening, we heard about Lyn's picnic lunch on the beach in Maine, just to celebrate Peter's birthday, and how Ann had cooked chicken pesto pasta, his favorite meal, and made the ice cream cake he used to request from her on his birthday.

Mark and I concluded the evening by sitting alone on the couch and leafing through pages of Peter's baby book, remembering the little boy full of energy, eager and bright-eyed, showing early talent in math and science, exuding an easygoing sense of humor.

We had totally forgotten, until we read about it that night in his book, how he had kept a fingernail collection "that you hoard every time Dad cuts your nails."

O N THE LAST DAY OF FEBRUARY 2003, Murray arranged a conference call with us so he could report on the latest court hearing about our case. To prepare for the call, I went into my office, shut the door, and put one of my framed photos of Peter next to my notepad.

Murray told us to expect a trial date of August 4—the first firm date we'd had in more than six months. We were incredulous, slow to believe that the long process might actually begin moving again. Murray wouldn't know for certain until the next hearing, May 28, so we would have to wait four more months for surety, agonizing and wondering, holding travel plans at bay, remaining available just in case.

We couldn't just get on with life while waiting for the trial. It was impossible to forget the roadblock we faced, the semi-truck around the bend ready to dump a load of boulders in our path. We would continue to be tense and anxious until we knew the road ahead of us was clear.

Murray didn't expect more motions or appeals that would delay the trial date. Every motion so far filed by the new defense attorney had been rejected, including a request for a change of venue. The prosecution's case was solid, and the judge, from whom we had gleaned some sympathy the first time around, would be the same. So we remained optimistic about an eventual guilty verdict.

Two trials for the five defendants had been affirmed by the judge. Shahid's trial for homicide would be completed first. Then the two other bouncers, the manager of the club, and the owner would be tried together for assault and for conspiracy to commit assault. Shahid had already been found guilty of those two charges in the first trial. Murray wanted to separate Shahid from the other defendants because he thought it would be less confusing for the jury, since only one man was implicated in the actual murder. Minimizing the number of defendants, attorneys, and explanations would simplify the case, he said.

Now, in spite of a motion by the defense to advance Shahid's sentencing for the aggravated assault and conspiracy to commit assault convictions, the judge refused to declare sentence until after Shahid's new trial for homicide. We were all satisfied that the sentencing delay would help guarantee the earlier verdicts would not be thrown out because of double jeopardy.

The defense attorney had managed to procure funds from the public defender to pay for tests he said he needed for his client's defense—DNA testing on several pairs of boots, blood specimens to review intoxication levels, more opinions on the medical examiner's report. Murray doubted these tests would reveal anything new. There hadn't been any blood, he reminded us, so no DNA test now could be the slightest bit helpful.

Then Murray said, "The defense wants Peter's medical records."

"Why? Why now?" We were shocked.

"We can contest if you want," Murray replied. "But what would be the point? They are just fishing. We all know Peter's medical records are not going to indicate any prior injuries that could have influenced his death."

"Sure. We don't have anything to hide." And we agreed with Murray not to procrastinate.

"I'll phone Middlebury College and Deutsche Bank to have them forward Peter's adult medical records to your office," said Mark.

"I'll get his childhood records. He had one pediatrician his whole life."

Murray seemed to talk to us differently—more candidly, less lawyerly—than he had before. We'd gotten to know each other during the three weeks of trial in August. Now he even joked, so atypical, about being snowbound during an unseasonable New Jersey blizzard. Off the cuff, he characterized the new defense attorney as "North" Jersey, called him long-winded, mildly irritating, and frequently off the mark.

Murray was optimistic, so we were too. He'd keep us informed, he said, in his preparation for the second trial.

"Call me if you need to. If I'm not available, ask for Jackie." We knew we could count on her to take care of us.

Then came a bombshell: "A second trial could last twice as long as the first," Murray told us. Twice as long as three weeks? We couldn't believe it. Six weeks? In New Jersey?

"The new defense attorney is very thorough," Murray said. "He's not going to let anything slip by him. My case won't change very much. I'll call the same witnesses. And what I did in the first trial is all public record. But we don't know what to expect from a new guy this time around."

"Do you still keep track of Robert?" I asked. I often worried about the availability of that sketchy off-duty bouncer from North Jersey who so powerfully corroborated Pete Steinberg's eye-witness testimony in the first trial. Would the prosecution get him to come back again?

"Yes, we know where he is. We keep in touch with him. He's as-sured us he'll be back," Murray said. "If any of our witnesses are not available for the second trial, we have video testimony from the first trial that is totally acceptable as evidence previously given under oath."

Just before hanging up, Mark sighed and asked Murray, "When will it all be over?"

Murray replied what we already suspected. "I can't tell you that."

AH, THOSE MEDICAL RECORDS. I hadn't anticipated the pain of picking them up from the pediatrician who'd treated Peter since his birth. I was just in time, she said, for they destroyed pediatric records around the twenty-fifth birthday. The file was slim, fewer than a dozen pages. Copying it the next day at work, I felt sicker and sadder as I turned over each brief page. Peter and his life—flesh and crunched fingers and broken bones—were real in my hands. On the paper of that file, he lived. Landing on the summary of one visit, my eye caught the words, "Normal nine-year-old male." I grabbed the papers from the copier, went into my office, and slumped into my chair.

In March, skiing with old friends in Utah, I felt Peter's presence everywhere . . . urging me to go faster, to relax, to bend my knees, to pull in my arms.

On the chairlift together, Mark said to me, "You know it's the eighth."

"Yes, I know. Twenty-one months."

We both remembered the anniversary date of Peter's death, but we didn't feel the need to share it with anyone else. From the lift we watched skiers jump around the moguls—young and colorful and eager skiers—zipping and zapping, hitting the top, twisting and sliding down the other side of the bump, and then bouncing up from the knees.

"Did Peter ski like that?" I asked Mark.

"Oh yeah . . . oh yeah."

It felt like forever since I'd seen him ski. He was probably sixteen, wearing the long blue and aqua green jacket that still hung in his closet and the long-tailed felt cap, long since lost, that trailed down his back. I wondered if he'd be over there now, in the trees next to mogul run, leading the pack or following the others. I imagined that if he were skiing today, he'd be wearing a helmet, maybe a camelback—Peter loved gear—and surely some fancy mirrored sunglasses. He'd probably be dressed in all black—a black turtleneck and a black fleece vest, tall and sleek in tight black ski pants—and he'd cut a lovely figure in the snow.

At the top of one lift, near the end of the day, I noticed a bunch of skiers sitting at picnic tables, standing around, drinking beer, taking a break, enjoying a live band. A long-haired juggler walked among them, joking with and engaging the good-looking, athletic young people, at rest after a long day's ski. Near me, a young man spread his jacket on the snow for his female companion, and I imagined Peter doing the same. If he were here, would he be dancing? Would he be egging on the juggler like the guys in front of us? Would he be talking to that lovely young woman?

I thought again about Atlantic City, about Peter's mood that night. Had he been boisterous and loud? Or calm and friendly? Before I could catch myself, tears were streaming down my face. I couldn't bear to sit in the snow and watch these gregarious kids have a good time. They were all so carefree.

I got so frustrated with myself. Mary, why do you let your mind wander? When, oh when, will it get easier?

I've been asked if I have ever wanted to die. Other bereaved mothers have confessed to me their wish to die. My answer to the question, most days, is: I'm not eager to die, but I'm no longer afraid of death. Once I told my pal Charlie I wouldn't care if I got breast cancer. She looked at me with wide-open eyes. "Oh, it's that bad, is it?"

But the next day at the ski resort, while indulging in a massage, I thought about death. Since Peter's death, massage had been part of my grief therapy, rejuvenating, like pressure released from a steam cooker. The kneading and tugging always pulled pain from deep-down muscles, loosed tears from my heart and soul, and magically cleansed and refreshed my flagging spirits.

I lay as still as possible on the table and tried not to breathe, holding as long as I could in the depth of each exhale. This is how it would happen. I wished I could die, if only for one breath, just so for a moment I could see Peter again. I thought about how ingeniously simple the human body is, breathing and then not breathing, how easy it is to die. My chest went up and down with hardly a twitch from my diaphragm. I could plunge a knife into my heart, hurt for a moment—hurt no more than I was hurting already—and ease off into sleep. It wouldn't be so bad.

One of the moms on the ski trip, an old friend who'd known Peter since our boys were in elementary school, asked me if I thought more about Peter as in the past—what we used to do together—or his future and what we would miss of it. It was a familiar question.

"I just miss the life I used to have," I replied.

Sixteen
Birds

O N APRIL 8 I SURPRISED MYSELF by not waking spontaneously at four to go down to the dock as I'd usually done every month on the anniversary of Peter's death. Instead I got up at my normal time, and when I remembered the date, I ventured down the hill to my bench for awhile before I left for work.

It was still chilly at the lake. The ice was just beginning to thaw, and Mark and I were betting on the day the ice would finally be gone, just as we used to bet on that day when we carpooled with our kids. A recent wind had tipped my bench, so I hoisted it back up, sat down, and pondered—again—the absence of my son. Where are you now? Are you in the hand of God? Are you standing tall and straight and proud next to Grandpa Peter, Grandma Edna, and Grandpa Rondeau?

I see you smiling at me. You look good.

A muskrat was swimming near shore. And there were mallards swimming around chunks of ice. They knew how to get a jump start on spring. Signs of life. Spring was coming.

God's world looked pretty lovely . . .

I was feeling pretty good, I told Peter. When I got my mocha on the way to work, I left twenty dollars for the staff, my private way of sharing Peter, celebrating his generosity, on the eighth of every month.

W HEN ARE YOU GOING TO CLEAR the leaves from Peter's tulips?" Mark asked me. I nearly choked. Mark was talking about my latest garden patch, one of bright red Dutch tulips I'd planted that first fall in memory of Peter, my little Dutch boy. When I'd first proposed the project, Mark had discouraged me.

"You have enough garden," he retorted. "No, I won't help you." So I prepared the bed by myself and now, the next spring, Mark was looking forward to those tulips. In a few weeks, we would snap a photo of the two of us in front of the full bloom of crimson-flamed flowers and e-mail it to a few friends: *Greetings of Spring, from Mary and Mark and Peter.*

I had buried one of Peter's shoes under those tulip bulbs, the Bally loafer he'd worn for my mother's ninetieth birthday, the last time we were all together as a family. I had lovingly patted the soil over the shoe, that fall, and I welcomed the growth of new life on top of it now. But the tulips didn't bloom well because the spot was too shady, so the next year we would order new white cedars to extend the existing border and hire gardeners to put in the shrubs. I wondered if they'd find the shoe.

They did. Now the loafer sits on the surface of the soil next to one of the new cedars, beside a rock I placed there and among hosta I planted. I say hello to Peter's shoe every time I make the circuit of my yard on the riding mower.

Spring unleashed, finally, a bit of buried energy in Mark and me. On weekends, for the first time in months, we actually accomplished a few tasks around the house, cleaning up the yard together, hauling out the patio furniture, reorganizing the garage. I hauled the boat back from storage and we launched it by ourselves. We worked hard, but we also took afternoon bike rides and sometimes squeezed in nine holes of golf.

We discovered birds that spring, and early in the mornings we walked with our binoculars. One morning about six o'clock, we noticed a Baltimore oriole glowing in gold at the peak of the tallest tree, his brilliant song piercing the glorious blue sky. Imagine his view, I thought. Suddenly Peter himself was poised at the top of the tree, guiding us into the day, singing out to us in a language we couldn't understand, proud and gloriously happy, watching over us from up above. Imagine his view!

To be a birder, you have to live in the moment. If you don't stop everything, the birds will fly away. Birds are insouciant yet persistent. They don't care a whit for us. They flutter about our feeders, flit in and out of our big trees, sing a cacophony with little regard for our presence. For me, birds became magical. They captured my attention, and then flew off over the horizon to a world I could only imagine, the world after death.

People say you learn to see your life with new eyes after great loss, and bird-watching became one of the ways we redefined our lives after the death of our son. Mark needed to find activities he couldn't imagine doing with his son, like fly-fishing, or like slowing down to pay attention to the birds in our own yard and getting up early to look for the migrant visitors. Peter would not have birded—too cerebral, too quiet. Yet birding for us became a way to refocus our attention on the beauty of the world we found ourselves in, privileged, after all, to live.

On the day before Mother's Day, we joined an Audubon bird excursion along the Mississippi River. With the help of experienced birders, we learned to identify birds by sound and soon tallied an impressive list of new finds, including towhees, ovenbirds, yellow-rumped warblers, scarlet tanagers, and indigo buntings. As spring advanced, I was thrilled to discover many of them in my own yard. It was a bit like being the mother of young children again: when I saw a shadow dart into a tree or heard an unfamiliar note in the air, I needed to respond immediately. I tore off my gardening gloves, picked up my binoculars, and sat down on my bench to savor the sight of the moment.

On Mother's Day, a rainy, cold day not even the birds could appreciate, we went to the storage unit where we kept Peter's belongings. We went every couple months to search for a specific item or to simply poke around the boxes, intending to discard things yet stopping short after an hour of sorting and reorganizing. We couldn't yet part with those tangible reminders of Peter's life. We loved to touch the torn corduroys, the suspenders Mark had given him for Christmas, which he never wore, the handsome business suits the two had shopped for together, the huge, nearly new athletic shoes.

"I like to go through his pockets," Mark said. "I find stuff, scraps of paper with his handwriting."

Peter's possessions were the leftover holdouts of a real person, a living son, a life well-lived.

Mother's Day that year was lonely. I didn't feel Peter's presence, rather, I felt his gone-ness. And I acutely felt my loneliness and Mark's. Though we had warm chatty phone conversations with both girls that day, neither mentioned their brother. All that time spent mothering—those challenging but rewarding years filled with cries and screams in the night and hugs and pleas for help—seemed so behind me. They were tough years, but they were the best years. Had I only known how really good life was for me . . . known it then.

A few days later I stopped at Home Depot after work to pick up a new garden hose. Mark was out for the evening for business, and since I still resisted going home to an empty house, I ran an errand just to stay away awhile longer. As I was heading back to my car, a father holding hands with a son who looked to be about thirteen or so approached the front of the store. The intimacy of their hand holding took my breath away. Before I could stop myself, I went up to him, extended my hand, and said, "Good work, Dad. Keep it up."

Startled, he limply touched my hand. "'Scuse me, ma'am?"

I repeated, "Good parenting, sir, keep it up. You've got a great-looking son." He beamed.

I said, "You must be proud of him." Then I swiftly walked to my car, got in, drove off, and burst into tears.

I didn't want to go home, suspecting I'd be hit with a fit of despair once I entered the empty house. My neighbors didn't appear to be home when I looked for signs of life in their driveways. Then I noticed Mark's car in our driveway. Home was exactly where I needed to be.

"What's going on, Mary?" he asked when he saw my tear-streaked face. I told him about seeing the father and young son walking hand in hand and being moved to speak to him.

He looked me in the eyes and quietly said, "Oh, Mary."

Then he turned away and looked at the mail. I couldn't believe it. Was that all he had to say? I went upstairs to my easy chair in our bedroom and sobbed my heart out. A few minutes later, he came up, sat down on the footstool beside me, and initiated a chatty conversation about his day.

That was often the way it went. When I was in the pits, my partner couldn't possibly join me there. Rather, Mark felt compelled to try to pull me gently up, to try to lift my spirits. And it was the same for me, for it was too scary for the both of us to fall apart at the same time. Who would ever help us then?

Grief was such a whipsaw of emotions, even after months, and perhaps even after years. I'd feel good one day, then sad the next. Sometimes I wasn't even sure if I wanted to feel better. Grief's old overcoat was pretty comfortable, keeping me warm in my own world of preoccupation and self-indulgence. Though I'd lost the cutting edge that once made me want to tell the world about Peter's death, I still needed to talk about it. Friends sometimes seemed too willing now to accept my feeble "fine" when they asked after me, too eager to drop the topic or to move me beyond my life-altering loss.

Sometimes I felt abandoned.

Mostly I felt so different from everyone else.

If someone pressed, I'd choke up, and tears would flow, giving the impression I was stuck in my grief, crying all the time, every day, which wasn't true anymore. I could sense people saying to themselves, "Oh good. I'm glad she's gotten over that."

But I didn't want them to think it was so easy. I wanted people to understand how awful and how permanent it was to lose a child.

Lou, my therapist, said, "Gradually it'll be just too hard to deal with the pain all the time, and you'll begin to put it aside, reserve it for just certain times, friends, or situations." I understood in my head what she was saying. Friends I'd made who had lost children were showing me how to do it. They'd talk with me, weep with me, and then leave and go on with their day, scarcely debilitated by the conversation, while I might remain sad for some time.

Was this acceptance, I wondered? Putting the pain in a certain place and reserving its expression for certain times? Certainly not ridding myself of it or ignoring it, but wearing it more privately, harboring it more protectively? Perhaps not sharing my grief wasn't being totally honest where others were concerned, but it was more honest and true to my own self.

Seventeen
Waiting for Another Trial

I n early June 2003 we were awaiting a phone call from Murray we expected would confirm a new trial in August. Still in jail, the defendant,
Shahid, had been moved from Atlantic County to North Jersey so he and
his new attorney could confer more conveniently in preparation for trial.

On the phone Murray reported the defense wasn't ready for trial
and had been granted a delay. We were shocked. *He's* not ready? What
about *us?*

Murray told us the new defense attorney had secured additional expert witness reports, including DNA analysis on the boots of all five defendants and a new medical report from his own hired medical examiner, all
paid for with state dollars. But the defense attorney was holding the reports
back from the prosecution, and would allow Murray to review them only
once he had committed to a new trial date, which Murray would not do. He
would not go to trial ill-prepared, and he told us we would need to wait.
Murray said he expected the judge to push the case forward on the docket,
to exert pressure on the defense to submit the reports to the court for Murray's review.

"How do you feel about December?" Murray asked.

It was nice enough of him to ask, but what difference would six
more months make? Nearly two years had passed since Peter's death.
What could we say? It wasn't our trial, after all. It was the state's. Even
so, we had been counting on August. Some friends had been planning to
attend too. We desperately wanted to get it over with.

Peter, twenty-three; Ann, twenty-five; and Carolyn, nineteen, on our patio, June 2000.

Mark's response was, "Why not dodge the bullet for six more months? Why not try to enjoy August in Minnesota rather than spend another one in New Jersey?"

But we were both terribly frustrated. Resolution for us felt like an eternity away. We wondered how justice could take so long.

"Who benefits from such a long trial delay?" I asked Murray.

"The defendant," he said. "The defense hopes to wear down the bereaving family's will to see it through."

We understood intellectually, but we felt worn out and sad. Even so, we had no choice but to accept the delay and to depend on Murray to decide the best time to try the case again. It wasn't about us—or about Peter. The trial had taken a life of its own.

Meanwhile, my fundraising job with the nonprofit book publisher had grown untenable. I didn't feel successful, supported, or empowered. Asking for money day after day required guts and persistence, and I had little energy left for the fight. I wasn't a quitter, but, frustrated and out of patience, I felt I had done everything I could.

The thought of leaving, however, made me feel empty, as though I'd failed again. It would be the second job I'd left since Peter's death, yet another ripple in the tidal wave of the gut-wrenching, god-damned change in my life since the loss of my son. Was it ever going to get better? I went back to my therapist and whined and whined and shouted and cried, "What do I do with all this anger?"

"It's normal," she said. "What else would you expect?"

"How long will it last?"

"I don't know," she said. "Underneath the anger lies the sadness, and if you sit with the sadness long enough, it will eventually go away." I wondered where would it go.

I told my therapist I felt like such a failure at grief. "It's too soon to expect to feel all right again, Mary. When something like this happens, all the sadness of a lifetime comes to the surface," she said.

I was tired of fundraising, and I questioned how anyone could believe my sincerity when I switched causes so rapidly. I didn't want to dig up new donors or continue to soothe existing ones. I realized I was finally tired of working, and I was lucky to have a husband who could support us both. So I "retired"—which sounded so much better than "quit."

I wasn't worried about having too much time on my hands. I sensed it was exactly what I needed now. People around me were experiencing their own pain and sorrow, and increasingly my attention was grabbed by newspaper accounts of other young persons' murders. Maybe I could help.

But before I could help others, I had to help myself. I had to stop being frantic, forceful, like I was trying to prove something to the world and to myself. I was a lot like my son—gregarious and extroverted by nature—but now I felt ready to reach inward to soothe the sharp edges of my feelings. I wanted to learn to express my anger more healthfully. I wanted to sit with my sadness and my loss. I wanted to listen . . . listen to everything in the world around me. I wanted to practice being alone again.

Maybe then the pain would go away.

LYN GRADUATED FROM COLLEGE AND moved back home. We shuffled around each other for a while, trying to establish boundaries for our new household of adults. To Mark and me, it felt like Lyn was beginning to fill a lot of the space left behind by Peter. She got a job working on a garden crew for the summer and left at dawn every morning with a cooler packed with lunch and a big thermos filled with ice water—just like Peter had when he headed off to summer soccer day camp. And she came back home at night with dirty socks smelling so bad that they needed to be soaked in Biz, just like Peter's.

Lyn and her friend were planning to head to Australia in the fall, to work their way around the country for several months. In the meantime, it was good, if sometimes tense, to have her back at home.

Lyn got after me to put away some of the many photos of Peter I had around the house. She wanted me to give up the polar bear jewelry and the charm bracelet I wore in his memory. She was worried about me, I knew, and I tried not to get angry with her, but I often found it difficult to muster the energy. I didn't have Peter's knack for getting her to cooperate with me.

Later in the summer I took a four-day canoe trip in Northern Minnesota with a college friend and three of her own friends whom I didn't know. I had plenty of quiet time, paddling at the bow of the canoe, to lose myself in the all-encompassing sky, the call of the loons, the ripples on the water, the warmth of the sun. I let my mind wander. I just was.

I had hoped to feel Peter's presence on the trip, and I did, but with some effort. Mostly, I found myself thinking about Carolyn, even though she wasn't on this trip. In my mind, she was guiding me and my new friends on this trip, just as she had guided our trip shortly after Peter's death. Once again, she told me to spit through my teeth when I brushed, to put on the same socks the second morning, even though they were cold and wet, because they'd just be cold and wet again in a few minutes. She taught me how to stow my gear as soon as I woke up and how to start the stove. As her lessons came back to me, I burst with pride for her strength, her leadership, and her gentle respect for the woods. Again I acknowledged she was a pretty amazing young woman with skills I treasured more heartily every day. Lyn deserved more credit from me.

I myself had never gotten much credit from my mother. Expressing her feelings was not her strong suit. Though we'd come close to commiserating in the weeks after Peter's death, it was usually because I had asked her about losing her own son when he was two and about losing her daughter to suicide when she was in her thirties. But my mother had little to share. When I broached my feelings, she usually changed the subject. I yearned to be more open with my daughters.

Both of our daughters were home with me and Mark for the Fourth of July and the second anniversary of their brother's death. At their suggestion, we spent a day canoeing down the St. Croix River, just an hour from our home, like we used to do when the kids were young. Memories rushed over me. I remembered Ann, Peter, and Lyn turning circles in their canoes, hanging on passing tree branches, dragging paddles in the water. I saw young Lyn blowing soapy bubbles, content in the middle of her siblings' canoe.

That weekend we bought another tree for Peter—a beautiful, straight, five-foot scarlet oak—and planted it together ourselves where we would be able to see it from the kitchen.

For church, on the seventh, we ordered flowers for Peter. Later Charlie called to say she had burst into tears in her own church that morning, thinking of the phone call she'd received two years before. "I thought about coming to sit with you on the dock," she said. "But you've got the girls." Then she said, "It's your day, Mary. It's your grief."

Indeed, it was my grief. I hated to accept this solitary journey, but I was beginning to acknowledge that every person who truly lives will experience sorrow, struggle with hardship, and face choices, and one of those choices might include whether or not to dwell with pain, or to give it up.

All four of us got up at four on July 8. We bundled up in jeans and sweatshirts, grabbed candles, bug spray, newspaper and matches, and headed down to the dock. The morning was calm but cloudy, with not even birdsong in the dark. We sat quietly for a long time, and then crouched, one by one, to light floating candles and set them on the surface of the water. Soon five candles hovered and flickered near the dock. The girls built a bonfire. Gradually the sky lightened and big billowy clouds framed the first tentative shafts of early morning sun.

Mesmerized by the flickering candles nodding on the water's surface and the play of clouds in the starkly sun-striped sky, I felt comfort in the mystery of God's world.

I thought about the final hours of Peter's life. Because of the trial, I knew more about those final hours and could think about them now with less fear. I knew Peter hadn't suffered. I knew he'd been unconscious throughout the attack and that he had died well before being declared dead in the hospital at 5:07. Now, two years later, we four stood next to the bonfire, embraced one another in a massive hug, and walked arm in arm back up the hill to our house.

The following Sunday, Darlene preached on the familiar verses from Ecclesiastes 3: *A season, a time for every purpose under heaven . . . a time to kill, a time to heal . . . a time to weep, a time to laugh.* Her sermon focused on the words unspoken in the text—"in between" time—in between the birthing and the dying, the planting and the plucking up, the mourning and the dancing. "This is the time, the time in between, when ordinary life is lived," she said. "Ordinary life, with all its joys and sorrows."

Her words struck a chord in my stained soul. She was imploring me to look for the joy, to be as optimistic as a child, to see the beauty. Though she never said "get over it" or "let it go," I grasped her directive to stop thinking so much about myself and to begin looking intentionally for ways to bring joy and comfort to someone else.

Linda's pastoral prayer echoed Darlene's message: "Help us to give up self-absorption and illusion." Just what I needed, the sermon and prayer seemed meant for me personally. I realized I'd been preoccupied for weeks, indeed, months, by the tragic event of our life. I'd been worried on this, the second anniversary, about friends not remembering, or perhaps remembering but not reaching out to us. I hadn't wanted to be ignored. But listening to Linda and Darlene, I realized I had failed by not reaching out to others, by not connecting, whether short on time or motivation, or simply too selfish, it didn't matter.

Believe in silent prayers, I told myself. People mean well. Accept their good thoughts, their good intentions, even when you have no way of knowing they're thinking of you, even when they don't call or reach out. And remember, Mary, for a few days in July 2001 you may have been the focus of everyone's love and concern, but you aren't anymore. Life goes on. Think about other people. Think about the beauty in every day. Find ways to be open to God, to give back, to make a difference.

The next morning at three I awoke to brilliant moonshine shimmering on the surface of the lake. A strong breeze was sending ripples in glimmering diagonal paths away from the dock. Peering from our bedroom window, I was so overwhelmed by the beauty of the scene that I threw on some clothes, and, stopping in the foyer to grab the enormous bouquet of flowers we'd brought home from church, I trundled down to the lake.

I didn't shed a tear. From the bouquet in my arms I pulled one huge sunflower and set it on the dock. Then I tossed out the others, whole-sale, in one big mass, into the lake as far as I could throw them. I picked up the remaining sunflower, kissed it, and threw it out even farther. Good riddance!

I was done with self-absorption and self-pity, I swore. It was time to get on with something else. I felt a spirit-cleansing rejuvenation.

I threw a chunk of my heart into the lake that moonlit night. Later I wanted to reel it back in. I was so determined, then, and I thought it would be so easy. I didn't realize how much loss tugs at the heart. Grief can't be shed in one gesture, here today and gone tomorrow. You can't toss it into the lake with a bunch of faded flowers.

I ALWAYS THOUGHT OF PETER AS MY BABY," said Hans, our Swedish friend who visited us in Minnesota later that July. We'd seen him the year before at his home in Brussels, and we would continue to see him almost every coming year. The time he'd spent with us in high school was especially formative, he told us, because his parents had divorced about that time and his brother had taken his own life. Hans considered us his second family. Ann and Peter were only toddlers then, and Lyn wasn't even born. "I re-member pushing Peter around endlessly in the stroller so he wouldn't cry while you made dinner."

Hans was tall and still thin, in his forties now and single, working as an economist for the European Union. Since becoming reacquainted in the late nineties, when Hans contacted us again after finding Peter's col-lege website, I often thought how much he and Peter resembled each other—dark-haired and handsome, athletic, modest and soft-spoken, yet somehow imposing. The two of them had reunited for a drink in London just months before Peter's death.

At our house Hans stayed in Peter's room, swam first thing every morning and again in the evening, lay on the grass to dry, and water-skied as soon as Mark got home from work. He took our car and visited the neighborhood where we had lived and the high school he had attended.

During his visit, the two of us drove up to the North Shore of Lake Superior for a couple days of hiking. Just me and Hans. We stayed in a rustic little two-bedroom cabin at water's edge. We ate pizza on the rocks on the shoreline, played Scrabble to rainfall pattering on the roof.

I interacted with Hans, I suppose, much as I would have interacted with Peter, talking more or less the same talk from the same respectful distance. Sometimes I'd try not to talk, to leave him alone, remembering the space I'd felt I needed to offer my son.

I wondered what Peter would think of my relationship with Hans. I wanted to tell him, Don't worry, Peter, I know he's not my son. Hans is a friend. No one could be your substitute. I will not try to make anyone take your place. Hans and all your friends—Pete and Mac and Todd and Kris and all the others—remind me of you, and I delight in those memories. But these friends are not—could never be—a son to me. They have their own moms and dads. *You* are my son.

Eighteen

Change in Case

For several months a quiet civil process had been running concurrently with the criminal process. With some hesitation, we had retained a civil attorney in Atlantic City recommended by a local attorney friend. When the New Jersey attorney came to Minneapolis for our initial interview, he convinced us we had a good case for damages against the club, because all five men had assaulted Peter during their work shift. Everyone we consulted felt the club should bear responsibility for the conduct of its employees, how they were trained and how they responded in emergencies. They should have locked the door and called the local police when the patron, Peter, tried to reenter the club, instead of attacking him on the sidewalk.

We thought a civil suit for damages against the club was one way we might make a dent in the seedy Atlantic City environment of strip clubs, liquor-law violators and violent bouncers. We didn't want anything similar to happen to other young men visiting Atlantic City. It wasn't about restitution—no amount of money could have made a difference in our loss. But hitting the pocketbooks of those involved might send a message.

One day at the end of July, Mark told me he'd had a phone conversation with the civil attorney, who said we'd probably have to settle out of court. The bouncers and the owner and the manager of the club didn't have any money or what money they had was hidden so well that they were impervious to damage suits. There were no pocketbooks to target.

So we filed suit against the broker who had arranged the insurance for the club. We and our attorney would attest the limited liability the club was insured for was less than the value of Peter's life and the services lost in his death. It was all extremely complicated and totally dependent on the laws of the state of New Jersey.

In conversations with friends, we rarely mentioned the civil process. We didn't want to give them the impression we hoped to profit from Peter's death. The arcane particulars eluded me, though the civil process in general gave Mark, an attorney who understood the matter and expected recourse under law, an avenue to try to make some good come from our tragedy. We both expected people to be punished for breaking the law—criminal or civil.

One balmy September afternoon when we were scheduled for a conference call about the civil suit, I went to Mark's office so we could be together when the call came. An actuary, who would be part of the phone meeting, would present a long list of questions we needed to answer in order for the attorneys to put a value on our son's life. Waiting for the phone to ring, my stomach was tight. I propped Peter's photo on the desk in front of us, made sure we had a Kleenex box nearby, and took my notepad and pencil in hand. Such a sordid, pecuniary task: how much was my son worth?

We were expected to list the achievements of our dead son, point by point, so his worth could be calculated. The questions were simple, factual, and quantitative: What were Peter's athletic endeavors? What were his positions of leadership? What grades did he get? What jobs did he have? Did he help around the house? Did he bring his friends home? Did he ever discuss taking care of us in our old age? Did he hint at his future plans?

The answers were equally clear: He was captain of the Nordic ski team. He was on the A honor roll. He loved to entertain, and he invited tons of friends to our home. He was an investment analyst, and he spent vacations in Minnesota, and we expected he'd probably come back to live here. Mark remained amazingly cool, calm, and objective. He was in his lawyer's chair, after all. I felt inclined to respond like a mother, to elaborate all I could. Yes, I said, he played the violin. No, he hadn't played in any civic orchestras, but he had once performed a duet with his sister Carolyn for his cousin's wedding.

The phone conference lasted an hour. It was excruciating to even think of putting a dollar figure on the life of a our son—trying to make relevant the extra accounting class he took during one summer in college in order to get prepared for a real-world job, describing family get-togethers, repeating kudos from his professor on publishing our son's honor's thesis. We were drained.

Hellish though it was, I wouldn't have missed it. One of the second or third hardest things I'd had to do in the long two years since Peter's death, it was also gratifying. Both of us simply loved to talk about Peter's life. Mark gave the facts, and I inserted the sentimental details whenever I could sneak them in.

We billowed with pride as that hour progressed, rising above violence and death. For an hour, Peter was alive again, and when it was over, we sank as though punctured. Our bright but briefly shining star was gone again.

THE FINAL DISPOSITION OF THE CIVIL SUIT would occur in early May 2004. It would be like a bad burp with a horrible aftertaste, something I would hope to forget immediately.

All of us—Mark and I, Ann and Carolyn, Bob and Charlie—met with the New Jersey civil attorney at a breakfast diner in downtown Atlantic City. He urged us to try the specialty of the house, scrapple, which was potatoes fried with some mystery sausage meat, and he droned on and on without saying much. Then we walked a couple blocks to a squarish, two-story modern building where civil matters were heard. I clinked my heels on hard sidewalk in the morning sun, passing lots of black suits and black mock turtlenecks, and gold chains round necklines, feeling as though I were in Sopranos-land.

The morning was torturous. Mark and I took turns testifying in minutest detail about our son's "services." We were asked for the number of hours we spent with him and on the phone each week while he was in London, for the amount of time we expected to spend together in the future, for the value of stock tips he'd given Mark. When my dear friend Charlie took the stand, she talked about the companionship Peter provided his father and mother and the counsel his mother would need if anything ever happened to his father. We all bled on the stand.

And at the end of the awful morning, with a rigid formula on a tablet in front of him, the judge ruled on the value of Peter's life. The damages, paltry as they were, would have to be paid by the club or by its insurer. The judge was sympathetic to us for, we later learned, he had a son the same age as Peter. But he was limited, he explained, by the laws of New Jersey, which do not consider lost future earnings or compensation for pain and suffering. It was shocking—and grossly unfair—to learn the award would have been significantly greater if Peter had died across the border in Pennsylvania, or if he had lingered longer in pain and agony before expiring. Cruelest of all, Peter's life was worth less because we wouldn't have needed him to help us financially in our old age.

The process of the civil procedure sickened us more than its outcome. We should have known better. We felt poorly informed by our civil attorney about the pecularities of New Jersey law, somewhat led up the primrose path. We left Atlantic City for the second time feeling disillusioned by slick lawyers and our country's judicial system.

THE CRIMINAL CASE FOR PETER'S DEATH changed dramatically in September 2003—eleven months after a new defense attorney had been hired by Shahid, thirteen months after the mistrial, and twenty-six months, more than two years, after Peter's death. Murray called us to report that in the next trial, the defense attorney would present a new cause of death. We were amazed: all of a sudden, the cause of Peter's death had changed.

The new defense attorney would dispute the prosecution's case that Peter died from blunt force trauma to the head inflicted by an outside agent. The defense's own paid-for expert, another forensic pathologist, was prepared to testify that Peter died due to *Commotio cordis.*

We had never heard of *Commotio cordis.* Neither had Murray. He explained that he'd learned it meant the cessation of heart function due to a sudden blow to the chest directly on top of the heart. The blow would have to be delivered at exactly the specific instant in the heart's rhythm to cause it to go into immediate ventricular fibrillation, or V-fib, causing death. The defense would propose that the bouncers' blows were fatal because of a preexisting but unknown abnormality in Peter's body. If the jury bought the theory of *Commotio cordis,* the defendant would not be culpable.

It was ludicrous. Two different witnesses had testified they each saw five big guys kicking Peter in the head and on the sides of his torso. Neither said anything about the bouncers kicking him in his chest. Both

Pete Steinberg and Robert, the off-duty bouncer who had witnessed the attack because he was nosy, were in absolute unanimity that Shahid and Shahid alone had kicked Peter's head repeatedly and forcefully, even when he lay unconscious on the sidewalk.

Both Atlantic County medical examiner and the expert-witness neuropathologist testified in the trial that Peter's death had been caused by repeated kicks to the head and subdural bleeding into the brain stem. The kicks had caused his heart to go into cardiac arrest.

We were totally disheartened. Our frantic Internet research told us *Commotio cordis* occurred primarily in young people whose bodies hadn't yet fully matured and usually while they were engaged in sports, most often baseball, softball, and ice hockey. A kid might get hit in the chest by a puck or a baseball and go into cardiac arrest.

We were dumbfounded. This would be their explanation for Peter's death when there was no evidence at autopsy of heart injury? To say *Commotio cordis* had caused Peter's death was far-fetched, baseless, even obscene.

We shared the news with Pete Steinberg, who was by now a surgery intern; our med-school daughter Ann; Mark's sister Ruth, also a medical professional; and other doctor friends. Nobody could believe it.

Unfortunately the defense didn't need to prove a thing. In the United States' system of jurisprudence, the burden of proof lies with the prosecution alone. The defense needs only to sow seeds of doubt, to lodge a sliver of doubt in the mind of a single juror. Unless all twelve jurors agreed with the prosecution's case, it would fail. And after what had happened in the first trial, we didn't have much confidence in juries.

Murray proposed hiring his own expert witness to counteract the defense's new theory. With new expert testimony, Murray would disprove *Commotio cordis* on cross-examination. At the same time, he believed the previous testimony of the medical examiner and neuropathologist was strong enough to disprove the new contentions.

So Murray was in a quandary. If he hired his own new expert, now at the end of September, more time would be needed to develop his case. We knew he too wanted the trial to be over, that he didn't want to prolong our agony or his own, but only he, we told him, could decide when to go to trial again. Mark and I would remain interested if not impatient bystanders, supportive of the prosecutor. But it was his case.

Gerry just shook his head when we were out to dinner with him and Kris one night. Our friends had been so stalwart, and we could be completely honest with them. "How awful. Don't you get mad?" Kris had asked when we explained the defense's new theory of how Peter died.

Then, hesitatingly, Gerry opened his mouth. "You know we love you guys. And I certainly don't mean to invade your privacy. But how invested are you in a satisfactory outcome of this retrial? Will you be disappointed, will you be bitter, if Shahid isn't found guilty or if the jury is deadlocked again?"

Mark immediately replied, "I just want the trial to be over. I'd take a plea bargain tomorrow. I'm there for Peter, not for any specific verdict."

But I thought for a while. Eventually I said, "I don't know."

Afterward at home, still thinking, I realized I *was* terribly invested in a satisfactory outcome of a new trial. I *did* want Shahid found guilty of some form of murder. I didn't need to know more about what had happened that night—I believed I already knew as much as I ever would. But I firmly believed Shahid had caused my son's death. I wanted him to fry.

I had to admit I'd be disappointed if Shahid weren't found guilty. Would I be bitter and pursue the case relentlessly? I hoped not. I was too practical, I told myself, to beat my head against a wall for too long, and I hoped I'd know when to desist. Meanwhile, as long as there was a judicial process underway, I had to have faith in the system. It was the only way I could find energy for the fight. I had to believe Shahid could be convicted. Why would Murray continue to care if we didn't?

This was, after all, for Peter. He'd want me to give it my all. He'd want me to be patient. But when the end had arrived—whenever that would be—he'd want me to put it away.

I couldn't blame our friends for wishing we'd forget, forgive, and move on. Maybe we were pinning our hopes on too illusory a goal. But our friends were not in our skins. Their sons would be home again for dinner.

MEANWHILE, LYN AND HER FRIEND left to travel and work their way through Australia. Letting her go was harder than I expected. She'd be gone for months, over the holidays, perhaps through the next trial.

"It's okay with me if I miss the trial, but will you be okay?" she asked.

"Of course," I reassured her, with my heart in my throat. "We just want you to be happy."

That summer with her had often been tense. I think it was hard for her to come back to live in our household that still harbored ghosts of her deceased brother. She wanted her life at home to be the same as it had been when she was growing up, when our family was intact, when her hopes and dreams were rich with potential. She had worshipped her older brother, but she didn't want to be haunted by his memory, and she wanted to remember him her own way. All her sadness and frustration spilled out one hot day in August when she was home sick from her gardening job. She came out to patio where I was sitting and writing in my journal.

"Why are you vegetating?" she asked me. "What happened to the mom I used to have? I used to be so proud to have a mom who had a career," she vented with tears clouding her eyes. "What's happened to my family?"

She went on and on in an explosion of anguish. Then she said, "I feel like I lost my parents at the same time as I lost my brother."

I stopped breathing. Then I swept her into my arms and we both cried together for a long time. "I wish I could make it better," I told her. "I wish I could bring our happy family back together again." Finally I told her, "I'm so sorry to have let your down."

"I was only twenty when Peter died," she said. "You abandoned me, left me on my own when I really needed you. You kept asking me about my grief, but you never really asked me about my own life. I needed your help in making plans for my future, for after graduation."

It was true. I wanted to take back those lost two years, have her be twenty again, get another chance to be her mother. I felt awful.

Our phone conversations during her junior year at college had been sporadic. We often failed to connect, and she seemed rarely to call us back when we left messages. Curled in upon ourselves, inaccessible and senseless to anyone or anything but our own pain, we probably didn't try hard enough. She *had* lost her parents when she lost her brother.

We talked for a long while and promised to talk more. I assured her we loved her and implored her for her patience. I asked her what we could do now. But she said it was too late, she had learned to live without us. She had grown up and didn't really need us anymore.

Lyn has seldom spent more than a few nights in our home since that summer though she lives in the city and comes over frequently. I think, or at least hope, anyone would say we have a loving and mutually respectful relationship. With therapy, we've learned to accept each other's separate styles of grief.

She now often seeks our advice, especially her father's since she's studying law like he did, and she always teaches me something new about herself, about myself, or about life in general. I've learned what a huge heart she has, how generous she's been in supporting new friends who have also lost siblings and how loyal she remains to longtime friends. I'd have to say that in many ways she's become the glue of our new family.

W HEN LYN LEFT FOR AUSTRALIA, Mark and I felt truly alone. Ann was in medical school in Baltimore, and we wouldn't see her until the holidays, so we left to drive to Montana for a few days of fly-fishing. At Big Sky, we settled into the beautiful mountain-top home of one of Mark's clients, our first vacation alone, just the two of us, since Peter's death.

On the long drive from Minnesota to Montana, I caught glimpses into the abyss of my husband's sorrow. Not a man to wear his grief on his sleeve, he showed it by his choice of music. Much more musically in-clined than I, he knew all the lyrics. He'd be singing along to something like the Beatles' "Let It Be," or Simon and Garfunkel's "Bridge Over Trou-bled Water," and then he'd get real quiet. I could tell he was thinking about Peter, even if he didn't say so.

At Big Sky we worked in separate rooms until, in the afternoon when it warmed up, we headed to one of the many rivers and streams in the area. We caught some fish, but more important we caught the spirit of being together and enjoying each other's company. In the evenings we sat and read by the fire. We didn't always need to talk, and I don't think I even cried. We found some level of couplehood again, some peace in sur-viving, some faith for the future. It was clear, though we'd never voiced any doubts to the contrary, that we'd stay together in spite of a loss the sort of which causes many couples to split.

Mark didn't talk about grief as easily as I did, but he was just as de-liberate in his suffering. He still wore Peter's clothes. He wore a pair of Peter's good business shoes even though his feet slipped a bit in them. He worked out in T-shirts that bore Peter's name, and he always rode Peter's bi-cycle now, the one Peter had built himself for a senior project in high school. Sometimes Mark wore Peter's Middlebury biking jersey or his wind jacket.

He never said, "Look what I'm wearing," or "Peter feels close to me today." He didn't talk like that. But I could tell his grief by his eyes. Sometimes they lingered on faces when we encountered young men, especially one on a bicycle. Often he greeted them and engaged them in conversation. "How are you doing? Where are you going?"

He liked to attend the athletic events of his friends' high school sons. And his office was full of Peter—his face on his screen saver and in pictures on his desk and on his shelves.

About the trial, Mark was more rational, more intellectual, than I was. I told myself that as a practicing attorney, Mark was paid to be calm, collected, and dispassionate. He was bound to understand the proceedings better than I, even though he wasn't a criminal attorney. He could tolerate the fits and starts in the legal process, whereas I more often resorted to knee-jerk emotional responses. I liked to think we balanced each other.

Even on vacation in Montana, judicial proceedings did not elude us. We were well aware that while we were wading in the Gallatin, our case was being discussed in an Atlantic County courtroom. One afternoon Murray called to tell us he decided to hire his own expert witness to disprove the *Commotio cordis* theory, which meant the trial would be postponed until the following March. Meanwhile, Shahid filed for a public defender, his third new attorney. "Maybe his family ran out of money," Murray said. A fresh start for Shahid could mean even further delay.

That night I awoke sweaty from a nightmare. I dreamt Mark and I were hiking in a very dry and rugged mountain terrain. I was so exhausted, I was dizzy and couldn't see anymore where to put my feet. I was wearing Ann's hiking boots and just barely managing to lift my heavy body from one edge to the next footfall. Mark reached down and helped me up. We climbed holding hands. Then we suddenly moved into a new landscape . . . snowy and icy with caves and deep crevasses. It was very cold and getting dark. We weren't prepared, dressed as we were for an arid hot-weather landscape. We started to panic. Mark said, "I really don't know how to get out of here."

Then I woke up. I got out of bed and went to the bathroom, but I hesitated to crawl back under the covers. I didn't want to fall asleep again and be lost once more in ice caves with my spouse.

Back home after our fly-fishing trip, without a job and with Carolyn gone to Australia, our house felt startingly empty of life. I missed the hubbub of active growing children. Though I was no longer young, I wasn't old either, not yet sixty. But I was done with mothering young children, done with working. Time hung on my hands like a challenge.

I was still unsettled by the silence. I felt lost, not quite sure where to go, what to do, where to set my anchor. I still felt adrift on a big sea. Where would the current take me today? What flotsam would I find on the way?

I started by cleaning house. Every day for more than a month in some primordial frenzy to see and to touch, I reacquainted myself with every nook and cranny of my nest. I needed to learn my world as it now existed. I opened every drawer. I sorted and patted, reorganized shelves, even painted the insides of closets. I worked in silence, rarely playing music or turning on television. Sometimes I talked to myself. Sometimes, when inclined to be social, I called my friends.

Solitude gradually became my closest friend. I took long walks alone while carrying binoculars to look for birds. I knew I was circling in closer and closer on the hole in my life.

I finally tackled the piles on my desk of Peter stuff—photos, cards and letters, stories, news articles. I shuffled and organized everything and assembled loose-leaf binders and albums that now take up more than three feet of shelf space. I was trying to put Peter back together again.

I found plenty of Peter flotsam: dirty golf balls, old fishing poles, a jacket in back of the mudroom closet he'd never wear again, the screened bug house he made with his Grandpa Peter—I no longer needed to save that to show Peter's children. I kept the scraps of paper that bore his handwriting, evidence of his muscle in the pencil scratchings.

As I tried to find his life again, I often encountered his death. I cried when I reread the news reports of his death, yet I rejoiced in the discovery of every detail of his life. I probed cautiously for fear of shattering cherished memories, but I was nevertheless hungry to find more. It was like approaching a hot fire: I had to see what was burning. The warmth felt exquisite, but how close to the fire could I get before the pain of his death hurt like hell?

I could not have done this work earlier. I was literally propelled forward by the energy of my son's life. The process of remembering brought me smiles, for Peter took such joy in simply living. In the photos I saw his smile over and over, the hugs he gave so many friends, especially girls whose names I will never get straight, his joy in posing for the camera, his gestures to whoever was taking the photo. It was as though he were looking directly at me. "Hi, Mom. How's your day?"

What I called my "Peter" work, other bereaved parents might have called grief work. It was hard work, tedious, sad and joyful at the same time, sometimes waking me in the wee hours of the morning or seducing me in the midday sun. I was transfixed. It often felt more like "Mary" work—staying home, focusing on myself, walking and writing and praying. In remembering Peter's life, I was hauling myself past his death, skipping over the agony of the first trial, capturing the best of Peter's sprit and zest and trying to carry on his legacy.

Together, Mark and I finally sorted through boxes of Peter's stuff in the rented storage unit, putting aside a big bag of everyday shirts, socks, and underwear to give to Goodwill.

"Do you want this?" Mark held up a creamy white pullover polar fleece shirt that zippered over the shoulder. Peter had worn it often during Minnesota's winters.

"Won't you wear it?" I asked him. He was more Peter's size than I.

"No, I don't think I'll ever wear it."

"Well, I doubt I will." But I didn't want anyone else we knew to wear it either. So we put it in the giveaway pile.

The next day I took the bags to Goodwill. I dropped them off with the attendant, took my receipt, and drove away. Tears started to flow almost immediately. I ran a couple errands, but I couldn't stop crying. I kept thinking about that white polar fleece shirt.

So I turned my car around and drove back to Goodwill. I went into the warehouse, and I started to paw through the crates where Peter's clothes were commingled with others.

An aproned woman cautiously approached me. "Are you looking for something?"

"Yeah," I grunted. She backed off and left me to my pawing, probably thinking I was a some sort of crazy lady on a mission. I found some of Peter's socks and shorts at the bottom, but I couldn't find the polar fleece shirt. I dug more furiously.

Then another attendant said, "Sometimes they take the good stuff straight out to the sales floor." So I went into the store and rifled through racks of jackets and sweaters, but I didn't come across Peter's white polar fleece.

Back in the warehouse, I climbed on the pallet and dug even deeper, determined to find the shirt. My head was near the bottom of a crate when I heard a woman's voice from the rear of the building, "Is this what you're looking for?"

High over her head, in her up-stretched arms, was Peter's shirt. I petted it all the way home, in tears. Then I asked my crafty older sister to make the shirt into a polar bear. I placed it on his bed for grandchildren-to-be, the zipper that used to be on Peter's shoulder running down the bear's back and making a perfect pocket for treasure.

Putting the pieces of Peter's life back together again was an exquisite pain, and I was beginning to understand how both pleasure and pain could be twisted together in one big ball to gradually refill the hole left in Peter's absence.

Little by little, the hole refilled with love. I loved Peter then and always would. Because I'd love him always, he hadn't really died. He lived with us in love. He loved me too—through the grace of God. In faith, I lived in the knowledge of his love.

KRIS CELEBRATED HER FIFTIETH BIRTHDAY in early December. She'd planned a huge party at the country club with formal dress, dancing, and dozens of mutual friends. I wasn't totally up for a big party, but Kris was a good friend and I wouldn't let her down. A group of us had taken dancing lessons in preparation, and I purchased a new black velvet skirt and fuzzy black tank top with a thin crocheted sweater to go over it. I even got myself new velvet dancing flats.

At the last minute, Mark was stuck at a real estate closing out of town and wasn't able to get back in time for the party. After stalling for a while, I decided to go by myself. These were my friends, after all.

I surprised myself by having a blast. I danced with nearly every man there and even asked and led some of them to the dance floor. By the end of the evening I was dancing with my girlfriends. I was drunk without imbibing a single drop of alcohol. It felt like my coming-out party—my coming-out-of-mourning party. I danced until the band stopped playing.

Then, when I got home, still charged up, I soaked in a hot bath by the light of candles and the glow of moonlight on the snow outside my bathroom window. From the tub I sat gazing into the starry sky over the lake when, suddenly, I saw a shooting star. I knew it was Peter—applauding and cheering my success in enjoying myself.

"Way to go, Mom!"

Nineteen

End of Process

On January 13, 2004, two-and-one-half years to the day after Peter's memorial service, the case against Shahid fell apart. Murray called to tell us he no longer thought he had a case for murder. We couldn't believe it. No case for the murder of our son.

Murray had received the written reports he'd anticipated from his new expert witness. As we had hoped would happen, the doctor-pathologist-attorney hired by Murray had returned an opinion that *Commotio cordis* was a bunch of bunk. Even though there was no blood, the expert witness said there was evidence on Peter's body of trauma that could have caused death, such as the bruises on the side of his head.

But the expert witness also said he couldn't concur conclusively with the first medical examiner that Peter's death was caused by kicking to his head, and he couldn't rule out Peter's level of intoxication as a contributing factor. In an individual with a blood alcohol level of 0.209 percent, a trauma much less severe than the one Peter suffered might have caused cardiac arrest, he said. A bruise on the left side of Peter's torso suggested an injury to his left lung that could have contributed to his death, he continued. Even Peter's head hitting the pavement when he was knocked down could have been a factor. In short, the expert witness couldn't be sure why Peter died.

Unlike the first medical examiner and the neuropathologist, who had both testified in the original trial that trauma to the head had caused swelling of the brain and then cardiac arrest, this expert witness couldn't be certain this was the cause of death. Any one or a combination of factors could have caused cardiac arrest, which then would have caused swelling in the brain.

It got worse. When Murray took the report back to the medical examiner and neuropathologist, both key witnesses in the first trial, he got a new response. The neuropathologist held tight—trauma to the top and back of the head had caused swelling in the medulla of the brain, which then caused cardiac arrest and death. However, the county medical examiner who performed the autopsy and then testified on the witness stand that trauma to the head had caused Peter's death, changed his mind when Murray re-contacted him. Maybe, he said, he wasn't so sure. Maybe the new expert witness was correct.

So no one could be tried for murder. Murray could not argue that Tamer Shahid's big black boots kicking my son's head had caused his death. It didn't matter that in the first trial Pete Steinberg and Robert had testified that they saw Shahid, and Shahid alone, kicking Peter in the head. It didn't matter that two medical experts had testified that kicking to the head and only kicking to the head had caused Peter's death. The medical examiner had changed his mind and could no longer be a credible witness for the prosecution. Shahid was off the hook for homicide.

"If the medical examiner had filed this opinion at the time of the autopsy," Murray said with barely contained fury, "I would never have charged Shahid with murder. I would have charged all five defendants with first-degree manslaughter. Now it's too late. I can't go back to the grand jury and ask to have the indictments changed."

"How can your medical examiner say this now?" I asked incredulously.

"I don't know, but he did. It's highly unusual for a county medical examiner to change his opinion after a trial and after so much time," Murray said.

"Now what will happen?" Mark asked.

"I've prepared a plea offer for second-degree manslaughter. The order in the state of New Jersey goes murder, first-degree or aggravated manslaughter, and second-degree or reckless manslaughter. The plea is on my desk as we speak. I'll send it to the defense counsel immediately along with my expert witness report. You remember how lopsided the system is . . . I'm obliged to show all my expert witness reports to the defense, they get to see everything, though they can pick and choose among multiple expert witness reports what they want to share and use in court."

"How long will this take? How long can they sit on a plea offer?"

"I'll give the attorney two weeks or so to talk with his client and whoever is paying for his defense, and then I'll phone him to see where it stands."

"And if he accepts the plea, what's the sentence?"

"It's up to the judge, but the term for second-degree manslaughter is five to ten years, served concurrently with the five to ten years he's expected to serve for the aggravated assault he's already been convicted of. This plea bargain in no way affects the conviction of the first trial. That was for the beating. This is for death as a result of that beating."

"And if he doesn't accept the plea?"

"Then I'm prepared to go to trial on March 1. But it won't be the same. It will be a trial for first-degree manslaughter, not murder. The way juries go, we'll hope to get a conviction for second-degree manslaughter."

We were stunned, speechless. I was numb, blank.

Then slowly . . . slowly . . . I grew horribly distraught. No trial? No murder? I tried to catch myself, but I was sinking fast.

What did I expect? Justice?

Come on, Mary, you've been living in a dream world. The system is so unfair, so skewed in favor of the defendant, so totally incognizant of the victims—Peter, his family, and his friends.

"You know I've been praying for a plea bargain for two years, Mary," Mark said later, trying to be more philosophical, trying to get me to calm down.

"But I wanted the guy to fry," I admitted.

"It's not about us, Mary."

I was furious, and I had a new target for my anger—the waffling medical examiner. I wanted to call the district attorney, to write a letter to help Murray get rid of him, to call the governor if I had to.

"In the future, in a homicide, when there's not an obvious cause of death, we'll be sure to get a second opinion on cause of death before charges are filed," Murray had said.

"Great," I said. "How's that supposed to help?"

"Well," replied Murray. "We have eighteen to twenty homicides each year in Atlantic County. Only a small percentage of the deaths don't have obvious causes—like bullet holes or slashes. So a second opinion will help the prosecution in those cases."

So what! How did that help us now?

I was plunged back into grief and fury. I slung my arrows at all the bad guys who'd made this whole thing go so wrong: the medical examiner, the single juror who screwed the first conviction, the prosecutor who didn't excuse that juror when he had the chance, the judge who pushed the jury to decide, the concierge who suggested the Naked City, the best man who chose Atlantic City for the party, the friends who didn't get Peter back safely to the hotel—and Peter, for drinking too much.

I was most furious with myself for caring so much about the doomed trial. Why would I even want it when Murray didn't feel we had a good chance? The trial would be awful, and what would it accomplish anyway?

Our pastor, Linda, was right: "This trial has taken on a life of its own."

And I was the one who had given it life. I had pinned my hopes on justice—Peter's justice. I expected criminals to take responsibility for their actions and pay the consequences. I was brought up that way.

I wanted to love and honor Peter, to stand up for him, show the world he was a responsible, normal twenty-four-year-old young man treated cruelly by an evil bouncer. Peter should be alive and happy today.

For the first time, I understood how a person could be provoked to take the law into her own hands. How it could be satisfying to pull a gun out of a handbag in court and shoot the perpetrator. Now I could imagine that kind of desperation.

J ACKIE, THE VICTIM-WITNESS COORDINATOR, called the next day. "How are you guys doing?" she asked softly.

"About as well as can be expected," I said spitting the words out through my tears.

"We all feel so sad," she told me. "Murray feels so bad. He hated giving you such news. I'm sure he cried after he talked to you. He's behind closed doors now preparing to go to trial."

"Preparing for *our* trial?"

"Yes. He has to prepare in case his plea bargain isn't accepted."

"Oh."

"I'm so sorry, Mary."

It only made me feel worse to know Murray had to prepare for a trial he didn't want to do.

THIS, FOR ME, WAS THE MOMENT PETER finally died. Looking back now from quite a different place, I can see how keeping the prospect of trial alive was my effort to keep Peter alive. I just didn't want him to die. I took the trial all too personally and in the process had misconstrued our country's judicial system. I thought my son's character and the honor and righteousness of my family was on trial rather than the one-time behavior of a man whose degree of responsibility would be judged by twelve jurors according to concrete evidence, witness testimony, and some judicial formula. There was absolutely no question in my mind that Shahid had totally caused my son's death, and I had wanted maximum punishment for him. I didn't want to settle for anything less than revenge—that man had killed my son and hurt my family and changed our lives forever.

I would never have been happy with any outcome from the courts. We had done all we could.

Justice for Peter had never been up to us.

A FEW DAYS LATER, WE RETURNED HOME from a Friday night movie to a phone message that had been left at ten that evening. Mr. Ward, an attorney in New Jersey, said he had information he thought we'd be interested in seeing, information about policemen involved in the case and suppression of evidence by the prosecution for Peter's murder. He offered to send it to us; we should call him back. We called Murray instead.

Mr. Ward was the defendant's private attorney negotiating the plea bargain. A few days after his phone call to us, he presented the information to Murray in a meeting to which he brought his own private investigator and a three-inch-thick binder of investigative reports. For nearly an hour, Murray told us afterward, Mr. Ward referred to report after report which he maintained wove a web of conspiracy against his defendant, Shahid, in a plot to do him in, to make him the fall guy. The reports included patently ludicrous claims, according to Murray, from dancers who were only now coming forward, two-and-a-half years after the murder, describing the evening quite differently from the way Pete Steinberg and Robert had testified. Mr. Ward's reports implicated organized crime as well as Atlantic City's police department in his conspiracy theory.

Murray wasn't impressed. In his opinion it was a scare tactic amounting to nothing more than hearsay and innuendo. He said most of the reports wouldn't be admissible in court anyway under the rules of evidence because they were based on such flimsy sources. He wasn't worried. No matter what Ward tried to claim, Murray was certain he had the right guy.

"I won't be losing any sleep," he said. "And no matter how shady the associations of other witnesses, Steinberg is untouchable. He's so squeaky clean, there's no way he can be implicated in any sort of organized crime.

"It's just a last-ditch effort to get me to drop all the charges against Shahid, let him out of jail now." He refused to take Ward's bait. The following day he would ask the judge to set a trial date for May 3.

So, a trial was once again a possibility? I felt whipsawed. At the end of the phone call, I asked Murray, "Are you offering us a ray of hope for justice?"

"I'm not in the hope-bestowing business," he said. "My role is to look at all the evidence objectively."

So I tried to stomp out that flicker of hope. I wanted to settle for a plea offer, minimal sentencing, meager justice . . . and closure. I had, after all, just accepted the process as over, but now another match was smouldering.

"We're due some good news one of these days," Mark said. I didn't even know what good news would be anymore.

THE CONCLUSION TO THE JUDICIAL PROCESS came quickly. It was late on a Friday in April during a bike ride in Cajun country in Louisiana when Jackie called my cell phone to tell us a plea bargain had been reached. Sweaty and exhausted, five miles from the finish of a fifty-mile day, I pulled my bike off to the side of the road, took off my helmet, and tried to comprehend the details.

Shahid would plead guilty the following Monday afternoon to reckless manslaughter in the death of Peter. It would be a pro forma short appearance before the judge, simple yes or no answers. We shouldn't think of attending, she said. He would be sentenced later. Then we'd have our opportunity to face Shahid.

I wanted to get on a plane. After being in the courtroom every day during the first trial and after waiting all these months for the second trial, I wanted to see Shahid finally express his guilt.

Mark was ecstatic. "You know I've been praying for a deal. I just want it to be over," he told our biking friends as they celebrated with him and consoled me.

I felt like all the wind had been knocked from my sails. I had been hoping for more than two years that Shahid might get twenty or more years for the death of my son, but now he'd get between five and ten. I could only cry and wring my hands. Our friends must have felt totally helpless.

When the moment of truth for Shahid finally came, we were crawling through security lines at the New Orleans airport. Jackie called to report that the plea bargain had taken longer than expected. Shahid had admitted to taking Peter out of the bar because he was drunk and unruly, and he admitted he had punched him outside on the sidewalk. But it was another bouncer named Mike, he said, who kicked Peter on the right side of his head and caused his death. It was the other Egyptian employee who was responsible, he maintained. People had confused the two of them.

How that could have been construed as an admission of guilt worthy of a plea bargain I would never understand. Unfortunately, I wasn't there. I probably would have screamed. Somehow or other, Shahid had admitted enough guilt, so the plea bargain stood. The judge had rejected defense allegations of mob involvement or police corruption, and had accepted the prosecution's motion to turn Shahid over to immigration authorities for probable deportation once his sentence was served. It was done.

I felt so sad when I heard that ten or more of Shahid's relatives or friends had been in the courtroom that day, as well as the Coptic priest. There had been no one for Peter. Reporters wanted comments, and we weren't there. Peter had no one to speak for him.

It was all so anticlimatic . . . so poor, so meager a result, so little recompense for such horrible, gut-wrenching loss . . . inadequate, unsatisfactory, distasteful. I couldn't come up with the right words for why I wasn't sighing with relief.

I had long ago given up my *expectations* of satisfactory justice. I had even given up my *hopes* once I knew a plea bargain was in the works. But I hadn't given up my *wishes*, and wishes would be the hardest to relinquish.

A couple days later I woke from a dream with a sense there was a shopping cart standing beside the bed, a shopping cart full of grief and anger and frustration. I considered staying in bed, hunkered under the covers, but I got up. I got up to face pain, grief, and anger. I told Linda, my pastor-friend, about the dream.

"What do you think it means?" she asked me.

"I think it means I'm holding onto garbage, keeping the load nearby."

"It makes me think about checking out," she said. "Maybe you're ready to make your purchase and exit, to take the goods and go."

MY DIGNITY—AND PETER'S HONOR—was assaulted again in the newspaper accounts of that court proceeding:

> *A bouncer accused of killing a 24-year-old investment banker and Minnesota native in a melee outside a strip club pleaded guilty to manslaughter Monday. . . . Westra, who went to the club with a dozen friends for a bachelor party, was ejected about 4 a.m., reportedly for groping one of the dancers. The melee occurred after he tried to reenter the club. . . .—John Curran, Associated Press, Press of Atlantic City, 4-20-04*

I thought I had gotten past my embarrassment over my doubts about Peter's behavior.

But now our friends were reading the newspapers and perhaps wondering again, Did he really grope the dancers?

Why was this never-substantiated point still news? Was it just an effort to justify the attack, explain the inexplicable? I just had to e-mail Pete Steinberg for his take. I asked specifically: *Did Peter pull on G-strings inside the club? Tell me, Pete. You don't need to protect us.*

Steinberg responded immediately:

I don't pay much attention to the press, and fortunately, I don't think most of the public does either. If the public's interest in this story spanned longer than a day I would be more concerned. . . . Peter was the same as the rest of us. He certainly wasn't hitting on any of the dancers that I knew of, and that wouldn't be his type of activity. In a different setting he would flirt with plenty of girls, but not with the dancers at a strip club. . . .

Give it up, Mary. Push the garbage cart away. Push it all the way back to New Jersey. Think about Peter's life, about our family, about the joy we shared.

"You can do it, Mom."

Twenty

Sentencing

At the end of May in 2004, we went back to New Jersey for Shahid's sentencing in the murder of Peter—Mark and I, Ann and Carolyn, our friends Bob and Charlie, Pete Steinberg, and more than twenty of Peter's friends, who were now our friends too. Under the terms of the plea agreement, the earlier convictions for conspiracy to commit aggravated assault and aggravated assault were now merged into the guilty plea to reckless manslaughter. He could get up to ten years in the New Jersey State Prison.

A packet of forty letters urging the maximum sentence possible had already been distributed to the judge and the defense. We crowded the small antechamber in the new courthouse, standing by quietly, not saying much, for more than an hour. The former pastor who'd been with us during jury deliberations, nearly two years before, was back with us again. I wanted to ask him for a group prayer but hadn't cleared the idea with my family, so I prayed silently to myself. Then Jackie walked us into the courtroom. Our family of four took seats on the bench behind Murray.

Shahid entered the courtroom in shackles and an orange jumpsuit. Still broad-shouldered and beefy, he now had a goatee and jet-black hair shaved close to his head. He looked solid, and he seemed to scowl and frown.

The defense went first, and then the prosecution, elaborating at length on the set formula of several aggravating and mitigating circumstances that the judge by law was obliged to consider. It was complicated. Mitigating circumstances included the fact that it was Shahid's first offense; the crime wasn't premeditated; he'd already been imprisoned for two years; he would likely respond well to probation. Aggravating circumstances included the brutality of the attack; the fact that Shahid had been involved in other altercations in jail; the contention that he'd pose a risk to society if released too soon.

Finally, we took our turns addressing the court. Ann went first, barely audible through her tears. I prayed she'd have strength to finish, and of course she did: "Three years later I miss Peter deeply. I miss who he was and who he would have become. I miss sharing *his* life with him and I miss sharing *my* life with him."

I prayed God would give me anger rather than tears. Carrie, one of Peter's friends, had urged me on, saying, "Anger has its power."

I felt strong when I stood up after Ann sat down. Stepping close to the defense table, I faced Shahid and flashed an eight by eleven photo from my mother's birthday. "This is my family. We used to be five. Now we're four. You made the hole." I hadn't noticed, but Charlie told me later that Shahid shook his head, wiped away tears, and mumbled, "I didn't do it. I didn't do it."

"I hope, Mr. Shahid, that you might one day have a son . . . I hope your son will remind you every day of what you took from us—in the line of your employment, in a moment of rage, with your big black boots. And you haven't even shown the decency of explaining why!"

When I took my seat Pete Steinberg grabbed my hand and clung to it through Lyn's statement. She was stoic and clear. "Peter Westra, drunk or sober, was not violent, and he was never disrespectful toward women. Anyone who says otherwise either never had the pleasure of meeting my brother, or is lying." She too faced Shahid. "I hope you have a good life. I really do. I've lived through enough pain to never wish it on anyone." But she elicited the ire of the judge, which I had probably provoked.

"Young lady, this isn't an occasion to enter into discussion with the persons involved, but rather a time to address the court."

The "court" was the judge. So she calmly took two steps toward the judge and without a blip changed all second-person pronouns to the third: "He pushed Peter to the ground," she said directly to the judge. "He kicked him until he lost consciousness, then he kept kicking until Peter was dead. I hope he has plenty of time to sit and think about that."

Steinberg too was calm and articulate. "We are left with his memory and the hollow feeling that an incarcerated Tamer Shahid is somehow going to make all the hurt and anger and pain dissolve, that a jail sentence is going to erase my memory of Peter dying in my hands. It's not so. That's not justice, but that's all our system has, and sadly, that's what I am here to implore the court to deliver."

Finally, Mark stood and walked forward. He looked small to me, quiet and sad. "I am Mark Westra of Dellwood, Minnesota, the father of Peter Westra. It is so difficult for me to understand what could have happened in the events leading up to his killing. We have heard many explanations from Tamer Shahid as to what happened that night. None of these is consistent with what our family or Peter's friends know of Peter. But any such explanations from Tamer, even if true, do not justify what happened. Peter may have deserved being ejected from the bar, we will never know. But none of Tamer's explanations justifies his beating Peter on the street . . . Peter being ganged up on . . . Peter being further beaten and kicked as he lay on the sidewalk . . . Tamer and the others walking back into the bar, leaving Peter lying on the sidewalk in his friend's arms and dying and not calling an ambulance.

"My religion teaches that I should forgive. I cannot yet do that. Too much has been taken away from me, my family, and Peter's friends. The emptiness in my life due to Peter's death will always be there for me. There is no room in my heart for mercy."

WHEN IT WAS TIME FOR MURRAY'S final summation, he faced the judge and exhibited more passion than we'd heard before. "What am I supposed to tell these people, Judge? They did everything right, and still they lost their son. Am I supposed to tell them they've been treated with dignity and compassion by our system? Am I supposed to tell them that I did my job? That I got a partial verdict? That when complications arose between medical experts over the cause of death, the state agreed to accept a plea to manslaughter—reckless homicide—rather than intentional homicide? That Shahid receives an appropriate sentence for the degree of crime to which he pleaded guilty? What am I supposed to tell them? The only thing that occurs to me is to suggest to them that Peter's life be measured not by the number of years in prison that his killer receives, but rather by the amount of love that remains in the hearts of those who mourn him . . . and that at some point in the distant future there will come a time when they can have memory without longing."

It would take a long time, and many readings, before I understood the consolation offered in Murray's words.

The judge sentenced Shahid to seven years. We will never totally understand or accept the sentence. Once the plea deal was struck, we never expected Shahid to get the max of ten years since it was his first offense, but we had hoped for eight. Even an additional year would have made a difference.

"It was a tragedy that began with alcohol, continued with anger, and ended in death," said the judge. Was this judge, a reformed alcoholic whom we heard kept a list of the Twelve Steps at his elbow, blaming Peter for being drunk?

Shahid had already served three years in jail, so he would be eligible for parole in fewer than four more years. Then he'd be turned over to immigration authorities and probably deported.

The press approached us afterward. I immediately said no to a video interview. One reporter, to whom I'd complained about the persistent reports of "groping," turned to me and asked, "Mrs. Westra, do you have any comment?" Though I'd given some thought to what I might say, I suddenly found myself speechless. I deferred to Mark. I've wondered since why I didn't seize the opportunity to express myself and to be Peter's mom publicly. I suspect I didn't trust myself, and I trusted Mark completely. It just felt like the right thing to do.

> In court Friday, Shahid and defense attorney William Ward insisted that Shahid had only a minor role in the attack, hitting Westra once as he ejected him and again after Westra fell backward onto the sidewalk. They said Westra hit Shahid first. . . .
>
> Westra's blood-alcohol content was above 0.20 percent, Ward added, and he said Shahid had thrown Westra out because he was pulling on dancers' G-strings and tops.
>
> But Westra's mother, father and two sisters . . . said that description was at odds with the Westra they knew as a peaceful, easygoing man who would use his ready wit to avoid confrontations.

"Peter Westra, drunk or sober, was never violent and never disrespectful toward women," said Carolyn Westra, his younger sister.—
John Curran, *Associated Press, Star Tribune,* 5-29-05

A month later, the four other defendants pleaded guilty in front
of the judge. The two bouncers pleaded guilty to third-degree reckless
assault. The owner and the manager of the bar pleaded guilty to simple
assault, also called "disorderly person."

Mark and I were present in September 2004 when they were sentenced. The bouncers got thirty days in county jail, eleven months in a
county work-release program, and five years of probation. The owner and
the manager got thirty days work-release time and two years of probation. Slaps on the hand, it seemed to us. The mother of one of the bouncers came up to me afterward in the corridor. She advanced to hug me, but
I stepped back from her embrace. I didn't need to do this, I told myself.
The Naked City, closed soon after Peter's death, reopened down the street
under a new name, but with most of the same employees, we heard.

In October 2004, we were awakened in the middle of the night
by a phone call from the county jail. An automated message spelled out
one of the bouncers' names in its wrenching entirety: "... M ... A ... R
... ," I was forced to listen to the entire sequence of letters before I could
punch in the code to verify we had received the notice of the defendant's
release from one month of incarceration. What was supposed to be a con-
sideration for our safety, so we'd be aware the defendant was back on the
street, felt, at three in the morning, like an intrusion.

On January 3, 2005, we received a Fedex package from the district
attorney's office with a letter. "Enclosed please find your son Peter's wallet
and its contents." Inside the worn brown leather wallet we'd given him
some years earlier for Christmas, we found sixty British pounds, a Minnesota Driver's license (6'2", 175 lbs, expires 02-03-02), an American Express corporate card, a British Network Rail Card, a receipt from Moshi
Moshi Sushi Ltd. in London, and Todd's business card.

Today his wallet sits on the trunk in the bedroom Peter used to
inhabit. In summer I put one of his baseball caps next to it, and in the
winter his ski hat.

Twenty-One

Forgiving

One evening shortly after we'd returned from the sentencing, Mark and I were coasting in the boat, roaming the shore, shell-shocked and numb, when our friends Denny and Sue, who were out in their pontoon, approached our boat. "We were heading over your way. Have you had dinner?" they asked. We said we hadn't. So they went to the grocery store for a roast chicken while I pulled makings of a salad from my refrigerator. A half hour later we convened on our patio with a cobbled dinner for four.

"So how are you guys?" Denny asked. Mark told them we were disappointed and frustrated. I started to weep.

Sue embraced me. Gently, she whispered, "Forgive him, Mary. Forgive Peter."

I didn't understand what she was talking about. Why did I need to forgive Peter? But I couldn't forget her words, "Forgive him." I thought about them for a long time. Maybe I did need to forgive my son. Maybe I was harboring blame. Maybe he could have done something, or not done something, that would have made a difference.

There were, after all, several lapses in judgment.

For starters, those young men should never have gone to Atlantic City for the bachelor party. Someone should have done more homework. Someone should have known it would be too sleazy for their comfort.

They shouldn't have gone to the Naked City. While it was true the concierge had directed Steinberg and Westra to the club after they asked for a recommendation, they should have left when they saw the seediness of the place, the lap dancers, and the bouncers. Or maybe some part of them liked the shady environment, sought the excitement. Maybe they felt daring or emboldened or entitled to be there. In any event, Peter should have left when the open bar closed. Like all but two of his friends, he should have gone back to the hotel and gone to bed.

Maybe Peter did drink too much. Ah, I admit it—he drank too much that night. What I will never know is what Peter said to Shahid to tick him off enough to put Peter in an armlock and haul him downstairs, outside the club. That's the hard part—not knowing what he said, for he must have said something. I suspect it was an innocent comment, perhaps misunderstood. Peter's enunciation had never been perfect, even when he was sober, and he might have had a sarcastic bent or snide smile that incensed the bouncer.

I do not fault Peter for drinking. He was a regular twenty-four-year-old young man out having fun with his friends. And no one was driving that night. Rather, I will acknowledge—no small feat for me—that Peter's alcohol consumption played a role in the events of that evening.

Then there's the strip club, that lap dancing. It conjures such awful images in my mind. I had to google it to understand exactly what it is. It's a sex dance offered in "gentlemen's clubs." Depending on local jurisdiction, lap dances can involve the dancer touching the patron, the patron touching the dancer, neither or both. And Peter was hauled out of the club for allegedly touching the dancer? I wondered if the club had a sign posted: Don't touch the dancers when they dangle their boobs in front of your face!

I can hear Peter telling me, "Hey mom, forget the lap dancing." And I tell myself, "You'll just never know, Mary, and it really doesn't make a bit of difference."

The biggest factor, the one that would have made all the difference in the world—in Peter's life—is that he could have walked away. Once outside, roughed up, the bouncer gone back inside to wash his hands, Peter could have walked away from the club. He should have walked away. Steinberg had tried to get him to leave, but Peter Westra was too big, too mad, too stubborn. Peter Westra should have listened to his friend.

My son was determined. He rarely lacked confidence. It was his nature to stand up for himself, for his friends, for his beliefs. I believe that night he thought he was being mistreated. Sober, I don't think my son could have walked away from a challenge. Drunk, he might have welcomed the next battle. I had never seen my son drunk. I had no idea how he behaved when he was drunk. But I remember going head to head with him myself. I remember a tussle he had in high school when he had to be pulled away from the smart-assed jock who was razzing him. I remember his not backing down.

And I remember my own obstinate, holier-than-thou attitude when I was under the influence of alcohol. I gave up alcohol as a tribute to my son, but also because I began to fear I too could have a lapse in judgment under its influence, a chance I don't want to take. I must be available for my daughters.

Talking with our Bob and Charlie after the civil hearing, Bob had called the boys' evening in Atlantic City a "lark," and Charlie had said that characterizing it that way helped her make sense of the tragedy. But it offended me. At the time, describing it as a lark implied carelessness and irresponsibility and assigned culpability to Peter for the events that had caused his death.

Now I better understand what Bob had meant—that they were boys on a quest for amusement and adventure. The whole situation became just so grave. Peter was at play that night, until suddenly he wasn't.

Did Peter's faulty judgment cause his death? If it had, could I forgive him? I feared I could not, so I avoided considering the quality of his judgment. Murder was easier for me to think about.

My son was not an angel, but he was not a fool. Despite his Manhattan and London urban sophistication, I suspect that evening he was somewhat naïve. Just being himself, and being drunk, he probably had no idea he was offending another man, albeit one from another culture who may not have understood his every word. I'm sure Peter was oblivious to the danger he was courting.

Why was he talking to Shahid in the first place? Why did he grow so irate and try to go back into the club? Why? Oh, why? I'll never stop asking.

From the trial I had hoped more than anything to learn what had transpired between Shahid and Peter to cause Shahid to take Peter out of the club in the first place. Pete Steinberg's version was the best we had:

He was certainly irate after being thrown on the car out front of the club, and rightly so, since as best I could tell he was assaulted by Shahid for un-

clear reasons, if one existed at all. . . . He was definitely drunk, but he'd been drunker. He was certainly not slurring his speech or unable to walk, but he was drunk.

I began to question the usual behavior of my son. I looked through photos of his college years and noticed scene after scene of Peter and his friends with drinks in hand. Compelled to e-mail his freshman roommate, Joe, I asked: *Did Peter drink more than others?*

Joe replied the same day: *No, Peter did not drink more than anyone else. Don't be silly. Peter was a typical young-20's social drinker. I'd wager, without fear of losing money, that if you collected pictures of any one of us in college, there'd be a lot of beer-in-hand shots.*

To reassure myself further, I dug out one letter to the judge, imploring a maximum sentence, from Kelly, a friend who shared Peter's semester abroad in London:

I always felt safe if Pete was around. Not because he was a big intimidating "tough guy," in fact quite the contrary, but because I knew he could handle any situation. It was like having your big brother around to keep an eye on you. It was just his way.

W HAT DID IT REALLY MATTER WHAT PETER said that night to Shahid or why?

Still it grates on me, not knowing. I will never know the details, the words, the triggers for the violence of that evening, and even if Shahid would answer my questions, I wouldn't believe him.

Peter had lived and breathed, he was attacked, and then he died. He didn't deserve to die. No matter how much he had drunk and no matter what he had said, he didn't deserve to be beaten to death. I can forgive Peter for being himself, for being human, for being mortal.

Peter, I forgive you for your lapse in judgment. You are my son. I raised you. I was supposed to be the responsible parent, teach you right from wrong, correct you when you showed poor judgment or misbehaved. Did I let you down? Did I let myself down?

Ah, Mary, you've got to forgive yourself too. You did the best you could. You are not a perfect mother. You too are a fallible human being. But you are a good parent, and Peter was a normal, good-enough young man.

I blame myself for feeling disappointed with the outcome of the trial. I believed in Peter, and I believed in the system.

But despite my stewing, I still have no idea what we could have done differently. Would we be any better off if we had pursued justice on our own? Hired our own private investigators? Done a more thorough search for civil attorneys? Talked to investigative reporters? Made a stink of our own looking for the stench in the cesspool?

It's crazy to think we Minnesota-nice folks could have tackled the conspiracy theories of Sopranos-land. Taking justice into our own hands, investigating on our own. What would we be now, except more frustrated, angrier, less naïve, and more mean?

What do I do with these misgivings and lonely regrets? I wear them, I bear them. They are part of my skin, like a scar, a wound crusted over.

> *" . . . I shall accept my regrets as part of my life . . . But I will not endlessly gaze at them. I shall allow the memories to prod me into doing better with those still living. And I shall allow them to sharpen the vision and intensify the hope for that Great Day coming when we can all throw ourselves into each other's arms and say, "I'm sorry."*—
> Nicolas Wolterstorff, *Lament for a Son*

I CAN FORGIVE PETER NOW, AND I CAN forgive myself. But I cannot yet forgive the perpetrators of Peter's death. That was made crystal clear to me during my sixtieth birthday celebration with my family in Iceland. The trip alone was validation that dreams after tragedy can come true—for I had always wanted to visit Iceland.

We were on the banks of Godafoss, one of the most enormous and fear-inspiring of eery Iceland's countless, untamed cataracts, named "God's Waterfall" after an early settler threw his heathen idols over the edge upon his conversion to Christianity. I was walking on slippery wet rocks right up to the knifelike ledges that seemed to drop off to the center of the earth. Soaked by clouds of mist and deafened by the ferocious roar of the churning water, I was speechless, full of awe for nature's show of fury. I thought about how much Peter would have loved standing with us on those ledges. I could easily imagine his boldness, his daring in a dangerous environment like this one—perhaps even misstepping, falling to his death, and how much easier it might be to accept such a death. I could understand the wrath of nature, accept it more easily than I could the wrath of man.

I will never make peace with the atrocity of Peter's murder. It should not have happened—that vicious act of five men against one. I still implore God to tell me why he did not stop it.

And I have concluded, with peace, that it is not my business to forgive the five men who killed Peter. It was their deed; forgiveness is their business.

Perhaps I will, one day, summon total forgiveness, but not now. Meanwhile, I will try to remain open to the possibility. For me, right now, it is enough that I am no longer preoccupied, indeed, consumed by anger and remorse over the death of my son.

Twenty-Two

Remembering

To come through great sorrow is to be reborn into a new world, someone said. Everything looks different, more precarious and more dangerous, but also more beautiful. The foundation of my world had tilted, it had threatened to slide me into the abyss. I am not totally steady yet, but I have not fallen into the abyss.

It has become a matter more of will and determination than hapless fate. My emotions have gradually settled more within my realm of control. Aware in a new way of the possibility of danger in my world since my son's death, I feel increasingly capable of protecting myself from peril. I can confront risks, evade them, or accept them. These are for me, after all, only everyday risks: biking in busy highways, driving on icy roads, staying healthy, staying in tune with my spiritual core. I don't live my life on sharp ledges. I can only hope not to be challenged so again.

Time soothes all wounds, we're told. It's true, but not completely. My scars are permanent and my pain will recur. I don't believe human beings possess a natural resiliency that intuitively saves them in times of trauma. After the death of a child, parents do collapse, marriages do break up, and people do get seriously ill.

For the brokenhearted, grief is hard work that can't be rushed. Recovery requires sheer determination.

My journey through grief is like a tumbleweed turning over and over again on itself, getting stuck sometimes on a fence, rising sometimes above the chaff and over the fence to another field. Grief for me is feeling

At a toy store on the Jersey shore.

every ounce of pain until slowly the pain is transformed into new life and renewed purpose, indeed, a new self.

I do not think of myself as a survivor. My healing is incomplete. Rather, my grief over my lost child, though no longer debilitating, is ever-present, a part of my heart, another layer of skin. I am comfortable in that new skin, most days, but I will always struggle to accept it, and will always strive to love it. For the rest of my life, I will be living with Peter, and with myself, in a whole new way.

I do not think I've thrived. Through loss I have become softer, bigger, more compassionate to the suffering around me, but in other ways, I've grown smaller—or my expectations have. But when a friend tells me I'm doing well, I think, "Maybe so," and I want to do even better.

I no longer feel like I wear that M for murder. I can meet new people, engage in conversation, and deal with questions about my family. I can say what I want to about my three children and about what happened to Peter, I can share my story or not share it, and I can suppress the details that are awkward at the time. My smile feels less pasted on. Most days I feel altered but okay. I wear colors again and jewelry and scarves and sometimes even perfume.

I don't know exactly how this movement of will occurred. There is no brilliant therapist, no exotic vacation, no special friend that can rekindle hope from the ashes of lost dreams.

> *"I don't really remember the day I first felt that all was not irremediably lost. Was it a child's smile that awoke me, or a sign of sadness exposed in a place I didn't want it seen? Or a sense of responsibility? Or had I finally given up on despair? Perhaps I was simply caught up again in the game of life."*
>
> —Anne Philipe, from *Healing After Loss*
> by Martha Whitmore Hickman

It takes more than time to heal a broken heart. Parents who have lost children must make new lives for themselves. It takes incredible effort, and even partners are often on separate journeys with different milestones.

Mark and I accepted countless suggestions and examples from others. We made resolutions, fell back, and resolved again on our various pathways toward peace. Yet in the end we each followed our own hearts.

Our sense of purpose was different. At one time, my purpose was to bring Peter back, in every way I could, or to remember him perfectly. Now I strive more to continue living healthfully and happily in the knowledge of his love. Mark works hard not to be identified solely by the loss of his son.

We tried to be Peter. Like Peter, we took care of our health, worked out, lost weight, and got fit. We wore his clothes, rode his bike, and took up cross-country skiing with a measure of zeal we could have only inherited from him. But far from twenty-four years old ourselves, we grew frustrated in time with the limits of our bodies. Instead, we became more serious about birding and fly-fishing, two activities that didn't constantly remind us of the prowess of our dead son.

We tried to be friends to his friends. We met groups of them in New York City or at Middlebury and conversed over dinner with them in the Midwest and in Europe. We attended nearly a dozen weddings, were hosts at one when Peter was an honorary groomsman, and serve as godparents to one little boy. We even welcomed the first baby named Peter, a child of the groom who was feted in Atlantic City. Though we're still in touch with several of Peter's friends, e-mails often bounce back these days and holiday greetings grow scarce. That's appropriate—we understand—for these young people are now in their thirties, busy with careers, on the move, and starting their own families. Yet, every once in a while, we are blessed with news that reassures us Peter has not been forgotten.

A COUPLE YEARS AGO, WE RECEIVED this note on Peter's birthday:

> *I am thinking of Peter today, as I do often, especially when I am skiing, sledding, or doing anything that celebrates life. You are in my thoughts and prayers. Fondly, Jen C. (Midd '00)*

We had no idea who Jen was, though I vaguely recalled her name from a note at the time of Peter's death. I wrote back to Jen and asked how she knew Peter. She e-mailed me in response:

Peter was my first Middlebury friend. He was so warm and welcoming . . . he made me feel ten feet tall every time I saw him . . . I remember meeting up with Peter at a dance during my first week on campus . . . he introduced me to his friends—which was just about everybody in the room. He knew everyone, and everyone loved him.

Jen and I now maintain a frequent e-mail connection. Jen's a writer too, and we have helped each other through revisions. Through me, she's learned about Peter, the child and the teenager, and through her, I've learned more about Peter, the college student.

I had to write right away about your description of Peter's hair looking like George Clooney's. When Peter cut his hair short he asked me if I liked his hair cut and I said, "I think you look like George Clooney." He replied, "Who's that?" I can still see him touching his hand to his hair, trying to figure out if this was a good or a bad thing. I couldn't believe Peter didn't know who GC was.

When she read about driving Peter to college with a rocket box on top of the Jeep holding four pairs of skis, she e-mailed:

I remember all those skis propped against the wall of his dorm room. I asked him why he had four pairs. He said, "I'm from Minnesota, you know."

About Peter starting the Croquet Club, she had to tell me about being invited to play "snowquet" in winter:

The story took place on the same night of the semi-formal. I was back in my room, getting ready for bed, when there was a knock on the door. There was Peter, still in his dress clothes, wondering if I'd like to play a round of croquet. There was probably a foot of snow on the ground; I thought he was kidding. Little did I know I was dealing with the President of the Croquet Club! He'd already set up an entire croquet set in the snow on the front lawn of my dorm.

Jen and I have shared our regrets as well. I told her how I much I missed never seeing Peter hold a girl's hand, and she shared her dreams of Peter:

He was laughing and happy and everything about him felt as close and real as if he were here right now—I could even feel his breath. He embraced me, then looked me in the eye and said, "Our time together was more than you're letting yourself remember."

NOW WE ALL CELEBRATE PETER'S LIFE. Countless rituals help us remember and celebrate. Many are small—tipping extra at the coffee shop on his birthday, lighting a bear candle every night at dinner, decorating his little tree for the holidays, sponsoring flowers at church. Down at the dock, the closest thing I have to gravesite, I keep a flat rock bearing his name and the years of his life near my bench. I love to look at the letters in his name.

Other rituals are larger. Memorial events have grown with time. Middlebury College classmates have organized a homecoming weekend fun run in Peter's name, which we've attended a couple times. And his high school now hosts a Nordic ski event, the Peter Westra Sprints, each year in early December for 150 local high school skiers. Mark and I recruit the volunteers and provide the treats.

Getting outside my skin and my experience has helped me enormously. I've finally been able to reach out to other families who have lost children, especially if they lost them to violence. Sometimes I send letters to families I read about in the newspapers. Sometimes they respond, and sometimes they don't, but I know from my personal experience that making the gesture is more important than getting a response.

We've been contacted by people who have read about our tragedy. Once we received a phone call from the aunt of a twenty-seven-year-old young man who was murdered in Atlantic City, just down the street from where Peter was, and almost three years to the day after Peter's death. Michael too was there for a bachelor party, and though bouncers weren't involved in his death, our kinship with his parents was immediate. Mark and I met them once for breakfast in New York City, and his mother and I still talk by phone every few months. She told me, "Mary, I think of you every morning. If you can do it, I can do it."

LATE ONE EVENING AFTER I'd returned home from visiting Ann in Baltimore, Mark and I were soaking together in the tub. He was quiet, and I could tell he had something on his mind.

"Mary, I've got a couple things to tell you."

"Tell me."

I looked him in the eye as he started, and stopped, and started again.

"You know my associate, Cole? Well, yesterday I noticed he was limping around the office. I asked him what was wrong. He said, 'Oh Mark, you don't want to know.' But he told me he was accosted by bouncers outside a club in Minneapolis on New Year's Eve. He had been waiting for his wife, and when she didn't come out, he tried to go back in to look for her, but the bouncers blocked his way—he wasn't supposed to reenter the club once he'd exited. They got into an argument, and the bouncers threw him to the ground and began to stomp on him. He thinks playing dead was the only thing that saved him. Now he's got to have knee surgery."

"Oh . . . Mark," I sighed.

"He said while he was lying there playing dead all he could think of was Peter."

"Oh . . . Mark."

"But that's not all." Jerry, another of Mark's coworkers, told him about the assault on his nephew, who was twenty-three-years old, leaving a club in Iowa City the night before New Year's Eve. Coming out of the club with friends, Mike, the nephew, saw a young guy writhing in pain in the gutter, and he bent down to try to help. The guy suddenly reared up, throwing Mike back down onto the pavement so that he hit his head on a cement retaining wall. "Mike got up, walked home, and went to bed, but in the morning his roommate couldn't wake him up. He's on life support now. They're talking about pulling the plug."

"Mark . . . how awful."

"Jerry said he hadn't wanted to tell me. He said he thought so much about Peter."

I contacted Mike's mother. We talked often during the judicial process, and I drove to Iowa to sit with her and her family in the courtroom when the perpetrator was sentenced. From the witness stand she looked my way and told me afterward, "Seeing you gave me such strength. You knew exactly how I was feeling."

Recently I've become friends with a mother whose son, Adam, another Middlebury graduate whom Peter might have known, was killed in a kayaking accident in Colorado. She tells me, "I would not have made it without you."

Being present for other moms who have lost a child validates my own scars. I am relieved to know pain can be transformed into compassion.

TIME DOES INDEED GO ON. I bask in the comfort of knowing I'm in God's world. The birds at my feeders are my soulmates. In the winter I watch woodpeckers and nuthatches seek sustenance in the bare brown branches of the huge oak outside my window. I listen for birdsong and welcome the stragglers back in spring. Nest here, I urge them, in this yard. Bring more life back to this grassy hillside.

I can't wait to work again in the yard—to plant flowers, ride the mower, sit on the dock. In June I know the exact days I must watch for the wood ducks. Two years ago, right in front of my tractor, I saw twelve baby wood ducks jump from Mark's birdhouse in the big oak tree, down to our lawn. From a height of twenty feet, little balls of wood-duck fluff toppled out through the hole, one after the other, and bounced in the grass, stretched out their winglets, lined up behind their mother, and waddled down the hill toward the lake. I captured two minutes of nature's drama.

Someone is watching over me. It must be Peter in God's playground. My faith sustains me and makes me want to continue to live and to breathe and even to thrive. I live daily in the conviction that I am loved by God.

Grief a spiritual journey. Indeed, every day of life is a spiritual journey. But these days I'm more inclined to mouth the words of Pierre Teilhard de Chardin: "We're not human beings on a spiritual journey, we are spiritual beings on a human journey." I had not known I was a spiritual being until I experienced grief. My faith, sorely tested, has been redoubled. Because God loves me and did not abandon me, I will not abandon life. Nebulous, loving grace carries me over the bridge from the past to the future, from loss to fullness, from hurting to helping.

On a chilly February morning, I don hat and mittens and affix a pedometer to my belt. I can see my breath in the early morning frosty air. Outside I'm greeted by a big and bold pileated woodpecker flying onto the trunk of the old oak. He flicks his red-tufted head, spreads his fan of white-tipped feathers and tail, and squawks loud enough to wake the neighbors. On the golf course, as I do my laps, my footprints leave dark tracks in the crispy glistening grass. I encounter a young buck, standing stock still, watching me even as I stop and talk to him. He continues to watch me when I walk past him, and then he turns, points his white tail to the sky, and dashes into the woods.

I head down to the lake. And even though the wooden planks of the dock are still piled at the shoreline and snowy ice blankets the water, I feel Peter's presence. Beneath the ice, the lake is alive. As surely as the sun will set and rise again tomorrow, the night full of the hoots of owls, I know the ducks and geese and loons will float again in the thawed lake. My garden will bloom, the grass will green. Accepting Peter's love and God's love, I trust things will be all right. Life settles down, surprises us, unsettles and rewards us, and goes on.

I am fortunate. I never expected to be able to say that. I lost my son, but I am fortunate. I am grateful for his twenty-four years. I am grateful for his life and for his love, which will not die. I say this now with honesty and optimism. Mark and I live in the love for and from our son.

Mark often says that he too has been fortunate. He did not fall into the abyss either. He is engaged in a career he loves, he feels successful, and he works with clients who are also his best friends.

We have our beloved daughters, thank God. We work hard to stay connected, to help them, and to cheer their activities and accomplishments. We have health, and more important, we have energy . . . energy emanating through us from our love for Peter.

Of course, we'd give up our gratitude in a second, even our health and our energy—just about anything—to get our son back again. But we can't.

We focus on joy, not sorrow, at least not usually, at least not often. Now, almost always, we choose to focus on Peter's life rather than on his death. Peter's buoyant personality, his joy for life, his spirit are in the air we breathe, the fabric we wear, the sweat on our brows, the flame of a candle at dinner, the gaze of a deer, the call of the loon. Peter's spirit is in all the relationships we hold dear, our love for our daughters, Ann and Carolyn, our love for each other, and our faith for the future.

We are guided by hope, the elusive thread that binds us to what once was and what might be again some day. Hope is the assurance that God is with us on every step of our journey, when we need him, and even when we think we can fly without him. In hope we heal and in hope we reach out to others who hurt. In hope we are confident that one glorious day we will be reunited in everlasting life with all of our loved ones.

I DREAMED OF PETER. IN THE DREAM he's been away on a very long cruise. I walk into a room resembling our kitchen where Lyn stands and leans her elbows on the wide counter and Ann sits on a stool with a notebook. Next to the counter, Mark stands with his arm around Peter. He exclaims, "Look who's come back!" Peter is thirty-two years old, tall, smiling, and handsome, with his dark brown hair smoothed back, and patches of gray showing over his ears. He's wearing a blue dress shirt, a loose leathery jacket, blue jeans, and hiking boots. He looks calm and content, confident, as though he's traveled around the globe several times on a trip for both business and for pleasure. We hug each other without tears. And, without apology or explanation, Peter says he's glad to see us.

That's how I think of Peter now—off on a long cruise, working and enjoying himself, somewhere beyond the horizon, taking in the magnificent wonders of a world I cannot imagine. From time to time he comes back to check on us, and he loves us always.

About the Author

Mary Rondeau Westra graduated from Macalester College. She has been a teacher, mother, La Leche League leader, marathon runner, Master Gardener, fundraiser for the arts, and museum volunteer guide. She lives with her husband, Mark, in White Bear Lake, Minnesota. Learn more at www.mwestra.com.

Acknowledgements

I am grateful for the many people who have helped make this book a reality. Friends and acquaintances reached out in the early months after my son's death to help care for me and my family. Others, by staying close and listening, helped shape this story of recovery.

Charlie Zylstra, my soul-sister, gave me the first journal after Peter's death and encouraged me to pour out my heart on the page. When eight journals gradually morphed into manuscripts, she read draft after draft—cheering, cajoling, and occasionally chiding me, always with patience and compassion. I am eternally grateful for the support she has shown then and since for me and my family.

Rob Anderson, a fellow traveler who's lost his own child, taught me that Peter always *is* and persuaded me I had a story worth sharing.

My teaching buddy and writing "coach" Stephen Schwandt encouraged me over and over when I was tempted to give up.

Early readers Dudley Riggle, Marty Wright, Ben Barnhardt, Tom Diffley, and Patricia Francisco Weaver gave helpful and much-needed advice. The Loft Center for Writers provided a supportive forum for working on craft, and instructors Nancy Raeburn, Mary Jean Port, Mary Carroll Moore, and Elizabeth Jarrett Andrew inspired and helped mold the book. The Minnesota State Arts Board "Art of Healing" exhibition showcased my early samples. My writers' group, Judy Krauss, Pat Spaulding, and Astrid Slungaard, patiently read and responded to draft after draft.

Thanks to Laurie Buss Herrmann for meticulous editing. And to Seal Dwyer and North Star Press for believing in my ability to reach a wide audience.

To Jen Crystal I extend a huge *merci* for coaxing me through one difficult revision and for never failing to believe in the value of this story. I'm grateful to Peter Steinberg for vetting the details and being our friend still, and to Mac, Petra, Robby, Deana and Peter's other friends for continuing to provide us glimpses of the person our son might have become. Special thanks to Rowan Morris for her World Trade Center photograph and to Mary Howard O'Brien for her portrait of Peter.

I would not be the same person today without my pastors, Linda Loving and Darlene Stensby, who remain my dear friends. They demonstrated love from God even before I knew myself to be a child of God. Thanks to many compassionate souls who listened to me over coffee, walked with me, and shared with me. Special thanks to Shelley Birkeland and Diane Haynor, who never allowed me to languish for long.

Above all, my heart goes out to my beloved daughters, Ann and Carolyn, who put up with hobbled mothering, yet bloomed. Each has her own version of this story, which I honor and respect.

And to Mark, my partner of forty-two years, the father of my children, my best friend, my better half. Everything is possible because of you.